THE CRACK-A-JOKE BOOK
Chosen by Children in Aid of Oxfam

How many jokes do you know? Lots, probably, but we are sure you don't know all those in this book. They have been sent to us by children of all ages (plus some adults) from all parts of the United Kingdom. Some of them may even have been sent in by you.

This is a very special book. Apart from being the 1,000th Puffin to be published, it is going to do something very important. As well as making you laugh, it will make other children all over the world happier, because all the royalties from the book are being given to OXFAM, to help them in their work.

Since 1942 OXFAM has been working with poor people around the world. To help mark the 50th Anniversary of its work, *The Crack-a-Joke Book* has had some new jokes added, and a new cover. It should raise more laughs, and more money for OXFAM's work.

Laughter does not belong to any one person or country. It belongs as much to the two children from Upper Volta, in the picture opposite, as to any other children. But it is one of those things that happens most often with children who are happy and healthy, who are loved and cared for, with a roof over their heads and enough to eat to give them the energy to play.

Too many children in the world don't have these things, and it is one of OXFAM's jobs to see they get them, so this is a book by children for children all over the world.

The Crack-a-Joke Book

chosen by children in aid of Oxfam

Cartoons by Mahood

Chapter headings
by Gerry Downes

PUFFIN BOOKS

PUFFIN BOOKS

Published by the Penguin Group
Penguin Books Ltd, 27 Wrights Lane, London W8 5TZ, England
Penguin Books USA Inc., 375 Hudson Street, New York, New York 10014, USA
Penguin Books Australia Ltd, Ringwood, Victoria, Australia
Penguin Books Canada Ltd, 10 Alcorn Avenue, Toronto, Ontario, Canada M4V 3B2
Penguin Books (NZ) Ltd, 182–190 Wairau Road, Auckland 10, New Zealand

Penguin Books Ltd, Registered Offices: Harmondsworth, Middlesex, England

Published in Puffin Books 1978
Reissued with additional material in Puffin Books 1992
9 10 8

This collection copyright © Oxfam, 1978, 1992
Illustrations copyright © Kenneth Mahood and Gerry Downes, 1978
All rights reserved

Printed in England by Clays Ltd, St Ives plc
Set in Monotype Ehrhardt

Contents

The jokes in this book have been supplied by children from all over the United Kingdom but this would never have been possible without the help of the following people:

THE GOODIES

Tim Brooke-Taylor
Graeme Garden
Bill Oddie

THAMES TELEVISION
Magpie
Tim Jones
Lesley Burgess
Jenny Hanley, Mick Robertson and Douglas Rae
Martyn Day
and all the production team

B.B.C. Radio 4 – *Today* programme

Radio Piccadilly, Manchester – 261m.
Radio Blackburn – 351m.
Radio Carlisle – 397m.
Radio Oxford – 202m.
Radio Leicester – 188m.
Radio Leeds – 271m.
Radio London – 206m.
Radio Trent – 200m.
Radio Tees – 257m.
Radio Merseyside – 202m.
Radio Cleveland – 194m.
Radio Plymouth Sound – 261m.
Radio Medway – 290m.

The Newcastle Chronicle & Journal
Oxford Star
The *Stage*

and Richard Stanley, of Oxfam

For the 1992 Anniversary Edition:

BBC Radio 5

Mary Kalemkerian
Mark Curry (presenter, *On Your Marks*)
Sally Beeston
Rolf Harris and Frank Carson, who helped

and Robert Cornford, of Oxfam

Foreword

I have always loved jokes. I loved them when I was very young and I still love them now that I'm . . . well, now that I'm . . . er . . . still very young. And this book is something that I have always wanted: a collection that is nothing but jokes, jokes, and more jokes. Some of them are old, and some of them are new – most of them are very funny, but a few of them are dreadful. Perhaps you are like me, and almost prefer the really dreadful ones, the ones that make you groan.

Because it is a book that I and my fellow 'Goodies', Graeme Garden and Bill Oddie, would like to have for ourselves, we were tickled pink when Oxfam and Puffin asked us to 'kick-off' their joint venture. Actually pink doesn't really describe it – we were tickled bright red. We began by launching an appeal for 'Your Favourite Jokes' on *Magpie* and, thanks to all who work on that splendid programme, they soon came tumbling in. Local radio stations and newspapers then joined in the joke gathering and once again the response was incredible. And that's why this particular collection is unique, for it has become an unofficial 'referendum' of the jokes that are loved the best. In other words, these are not the jokes that *we* are telling *you* are the best – *you* have told us.

On behalf of Oxfam I want to thank all of you who have contributed, with a special thanks to Kenneth Mahood and Gerry Downes for all the cartoons and chapter headings donated free – a particularly generous act. (Actually, one of the drawings is by Graeme Garden but I'm not going to mention it.) On a purely personal note, as a family member of the Puffin Club, I would like to say how very happy I am to be associated with the 1,000th title in their tremendous series.

Lastly I'd like to thank *you*, the person who has bought the book (if you haven't, rush out and buy one immediately). I think you've got a bargain, and hope you'll think you have, too.

Goodie wishes from all three of us.

TIM BROOKE-TAYLOR

Foreword to the 1992 Anniversary Edition

Thirteen years later, and *The Crack-a-Joke Book* is still the No. 1 collection of jokes. When we in Radio 5 were asked by Oxfam to help collect jokes for Oxfam's Anniversary we thought hard about what to ask for – and ended up asking our listeners to send in what they thought were the best new jokes they had heard. Then we came to select jokes for the *Annie Who?* section, and we found that lots of the 'new' jokes were already in the book.

I think this shows that not much changes in the world – and good jokes are good jokes all the time. Every person coming across your 'old favourite' for the first time thinks it's brand new, and listens with fresh ears. One of the jokes we were sent was:

What is as funny the second time round?
    A recycled joke!

Very true (and thank you Sebastian Wolf)!

Anyway, I hope you enjoy the jokes. Are you ready to start the book? On your marks . . . get set . . . and turn over the page.

MARK CURRY

Jumbo Mumbo
WHAT DO YOU GIVE AN ELEPHANT WITH BIG FEET?
why don't elephants eat penguins?
what's big, grey and mutters?
HOW DO YOU GET AN ELEPHANT IN A MATCHBOX?
How do elephants dive into swimming pools?
WHEN DO ELEPHANTS HAVE EIGHT FEET?

What is big, grey and mutters?
    A mumbo jumbo.

What's grey and lights up?
    An electric elephant.

What's grey and white and red all over?
    An embarrassed elephant.

What do you call an elephant that flies?
    A jumbo jet.

What did the hotel manager say to the elephant who couldn't pay his bill?
    Pack your trunk and clear out.

What do you give an elephant who is exhausted?
    Trunkquillizers.

What did the river say to the elephant when he sat on it?
    'Well, I'll be damned.'

What do you give an elephant with big feet?
    Plenty of room.

What time is it when an elephant sits on a fence?
    Time to get a new one.

What do you get if you cross an elephant with a goldfish?
Swimming trunks.

What's the difference between a lemon and a white elephant?
A lemon is yellow.

What's the difference between a biscuit and an elephant?
You can't dip an elephant in your tea.

What's the difference between an Indian Elephant and an African Elephant?
About 3,000 miles.

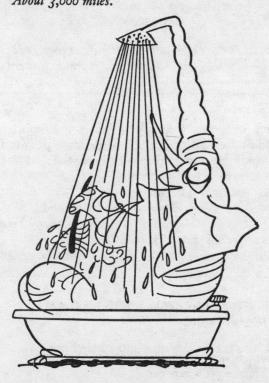

Why don't you go into the jungle after six o'clock?
Because of elephants falling out of trees.

Why do elephants have big ears?
Noddy wouldn't pay the ransom.

Why do elephants paint the soles of their feet yellow?
So they can hide upside down in the custard.
Have you ever seen an elephant hiding upside down in the custard?
No.
Shows what a good disguise it is.

Why don't elephants eat penguins?
They can't get the wrappers off.

Why couldn't the elephants go swimming together?
Because they only had one pair of trunks between them.

There once was a man who was standing in the middle of a road with a box of elephant powder in his hands. He was spreading it all over the road when a policeman walked up to him.
POLICEMAN: 'What are you doing?'
MAN: 'Spreading elephant powder around.'
POLICEMAN: 'There are no elephants round here.'
MAN: 'Well, it must be good stuff then.'

How do elephants dive into swimming-pools?
Head first.

How do you get an elephant into a matchbox?
Take all the matches out first.

How can you tell if there's an elephant in the refrigerator?
You can't shut the door.

How can you tell if an elephant has been in your fridge?
Footprints in the butter.

How does an elephant get down from a tree?
He stands on a leaf and waits for autumn.

How do you get down from an elephant?
You don't get down off an elephant, you get down off a duck.

When do elephants have eight feet?
When there are two of them.

Which takes less time to get ready for a trip, an elephant or a rooster?
A rooster – he only takes his comb.

Can an elephant jump higher than a lamp-post?
Yes. Lamp-posts can't jump.

What do you get if you cross an elephant with a bus driver?
A trunk an' driver.

How can you tell when there's an elephant under the bed?
When you're nearly touching the ceiling.

GHOSTLY GIGGLES

What do ghosts eat for supper?

WHAT DO GHOSTS CALL THEIR NAVY?

Who cooks for Dracula?

What do you flatten a ghost with?

HOW DOES A WITCH TELL THE TIME?

WHY DOES A WITCH RIDE ON A BROOM?

What do short-sighted ghosts wear?
   Spooktacles.

What do ghosts eat for lunch?
   Ghoulash.

What do ghosts eat for supper?
   Spook-etti.

What do ghosts call their navy?
   Ghost Guard.

What do you flatten a ghost with?
   A spirit-level.

What do ghosts have for breakfast?
   Dreaded wheat.

How do ghosts pass through a locked door?
   They have a skeleton key.

What do you call a play that's acted by ghosts?
   A phantomime.

What walks backwards through walls going, 'Er . . . boo'?
   A nervous ghost.

What did the barman say when the ghost asked for a drink?
'*We don't serve spirits.*'

What do you call a wicked old woman who lives by the sea?
A sandwitch.

What do you get if you cross a ghost and a packet of crisps?
Snacks that go munch in the night.

Why does a witch ride on a broom?
A vacuum cleaner is too heavy.

How does a witch tell the time?
She wears a witch watch.

What do they call Dracula?
A pain in the neck.

What's Dracula's favourite song?
'Fangs for the Memory'.

Where does Dracula get all his jokes?
From his crypt writer.

What's a vampire's favourite tourist spot?
The Vampire State Building.

What kind of boats do vampires like?
Blood vessels.

Knock, Knock.
Who's there?
Frank.
Frank who?
Frankenstein.

What's the difference between a wizard and the letters
K, E, M, A, S?
One makes spells and the other spells makes.

What did the skeleton reply when the bus conductor called
'Fares please.'?
'Sorry, I'm skint.'

CRAZY QUACKS
why did the patient laugh all through his operation?
"DOCTOR, DOCTOR, I think I'm a clock!"
who is known as the chiropodist King?
WHAT LETTERS ARE BAD FOR YOUR TEETH?
what do the dentist and the farmer have in common?
"DOCTOR, DOCTOR, I FEEL LIKE A SPOON!"

'Doctor, doctor, I feel like a pair of curtains.'
    'Well, pull yourself together then.'

'Doctor, doctor, I keep thinking I'm invisible.'
    'Who said that?'

'Doctor, doctor, I feel like a billiard ball.'
    'Well, get to the back of the queue.'

'Doctor, doctor, I feel like a five-pound note.'
    'Go shopping, the change will do you good.'

'Doctor, doctor, I feel like a spoon.'
    'Sit down and don't stir.'

'Doctor, doctor, I feel like a pack of cards.'
    'Sit down and I'll deal with you later.'

'Doctor, doctor, I keep seeing little black spots before my eyes.'
'Have you seen a doctor before?'
'No, just little black spots.'

'Doctor, doctor, I can't get to sleep at night.'
    'Lie on the end of the bed and you'll soon drop off.'

'Doctor, doctor, I've just swallowed a sheep.'
'How do you feel?'
'Very ba-a-a-ad.'

DOCTOR: 'You need glasses.'
PATIENT: 'How did you know?'
DOCTOR: 'I could tell as soon as you walked through
   the window.'

'Doctor, doctor, what can I do, my little boy has swallowed
   my pen?'
   Use a pencil till I get there.

'Doctor, doctor, everyone thinks I'm a liar.'
   I don't believe you.

'Doctor, my family think I'm mad.'
'Why?'
'Because I like sausages.'
'Nonsense, I like sausages too.'
'You do? You must come round and see my collection. I have hundreds.'

PATIENT: 'Doctor, doctor, everyone keeps being rude to me.'
DOCTOR: 'Get out of here you silly fool.'

'Doctor, doctor, I keep thinking there's two of me.'
'One at a time please.'

DOCTOR: 'Mr Beazley, that pain in your leg is simply due to old age.'
MR B: 'Well, my other leg is just as old and that doesn't hurt.'

FIRST TONSIL: 'What are you getting dressed up for?'
SECOND TONSIL: 'Oh, the doctor is taking me out tonight.'

Did you hear the one about the optician's daughter who made a spectacle of herself?

MAN: 'Ouch! A crab just bit my toe.'
DR: 'Which one?'
MAN: 'I don't know, all crabs look alike to me.'

'Doctor, doctor, will you help me out?'
'Certainly, which way did you come in?'

'Doctor, doctor, I keep thinking I'm a strawberry.'
>   *'Hmm, you're really in a jam aren't you.'*

DOCTOR: 'Did you drink your orange juice after your bath?'
PATIENT: 'After drinking the bath I didn't have too much room for the orange juice.'

'Doctor, doctor, I keep thinking I'm a bird.'
>   *'Well, perch yourself there and I'll tweet you in a minute.'*

PATIENT: 'Will my measles be better next week, doctor?'
DOCTOR: 'Well, I hate to make rash promises.'

'Doctor, doctor, I've swallowed the film out of my camera.'
>   *'Oh, I hope nothing develops.'*

'Doctor, I have a terrible problem. I keep stealing things.'
>   *'Have you been taking anything for it?'*

PATIENT TO PSYCHIATRIST: 'I keep feeling I'm covered in gold paint.'
PSYCHIATRIST: 'Don't worry, that's just a gilt complex.'

Why was the patient laughing all through his operation?
>   *Because the doctor put him in stitches.*

What letters are bad for your teeth?
>   *D/K/(decay).*

'Doctor, doctor, I think I'm a clock.'
>   *'Well don't get wound up about it.'*

'Doctor, doctor, I feel like a dog.'
'Sit down and tell me about it.'
'I'm not allowed on the furniture.'

'Doctor, doctor, I keep thinking I'm a dustbin.'
    '*Don't talk rubbish.*'

'Doctor, doctor, I've lost my memory.'
'When did this happen?'
'When did what happen?'

'Doctor, doctor, I keep thinking I'm a goat.'
'How long have you had this feeling?'
'Since I was a kid.'

'Doctor, doctor, I keep seeing striped camels.'
'Have you ever seen a psychiatrist?'
'No, I only see striped camels.'

DOCTOR: 'Do you talk in your sleep?'
VICAR: 'No, I talk in other people's.'

'Doctor, doctor, I feel like a cricket ball.'
'How's that?'
'Don't *you* start.'

'Who is known as the chiropodist king?'
    '*William the Cornqueror.*'

Why did the little girl skip?
    She had just taken her medicine and forgotten to shake the bottle.

Why did the little girl tiptoe past the medicine cabinet?
    She didn't want to wake the sleeping pills.

28

What do a dentist and a farmer have in common?
They both deal in acres (achers).

When my friend John King was staying with us, he broke his newly capped front tooth so he went to my dentist. The receptionist filled in his details as follows.

NAME: King, John.
COMPLAINT: Crown came off.

A Funny Fin Happened

How do you help a deaf fisherman?

What menaces the deep and plays the banjo?

WHAT DO SEA MONSTERS EAT?

WHICH musical instrument could be used for fishing?

WHAT'S A HOWLING BABY WHALE?

JIMMY: 'What's a howling baby whale?'
BILLY: 'A little blubber.'

How do you help a deaf fisherman?
Give him a herring aid.

Where are whales weighed?
In a whaleweigh station.

What do sea monsters eat?
Fish and ships.

What's the best way to communicate with a fish?
Drop it a line.

What kind of fish do you find in a bird-cage?
A perch.

What kind of fish is most useful on ice?
A skate.

What fish terrorizes other fish?
Jack the Kipper.

What lies at the bottom of the sea and is dangerous to man?
Billy the Squid.

What do you get when you cross a killer shark with a helicopter?
A Helichopper.

How can you tell that fish are musical?
Everyone knows about the piano tuna.

What menaces the deep and plays the banjo?
Jaws Formby.

What is pink, lives at the bottom of the sea, and sings 'Give me the moonlight'?
Frankie Prawn.

Which musical instrument could be used for fishing?
A cast-a-net.

What did the boy octopus say to the girl octopus?
I want to hold your hand hand hand hand hand hand hand hand.

BILLY: 'How many fish have you caught?'
BOB: 'Oh, I couldn't count them.'
BILLY: 'Why, you haven't caught any!'
BOB: 'No, that's why I can't count them.'

MUM: 'Tommy, shouldn't you give the fish some more water?'
TOMMY: 'Why? It hasn't drunk that lot yet.'

Where do fish wash?
In a river basin.

If fish lived on land, which country would they live in?
Finland.

What part of a fish weighs the most?
The scales.

'A boy bought two fish, but when he got home he had three.'

'How can this be?'

'He had two flounders, and one smelt.'

Why are fishmongers so mean?
Because their job makes them sell fish.

Conversation in a chip shop: 'A shark and chips, and make it snappy.'

What's the best way to catch a fish?
Get someone to throw one at you.

Why do people go to bed?
> *Because the bed won't come to them.*

Why is a river lazy?
> *Because it seldom gets out of its bed.*

Why did the man take his pencil to bed?
> *Because he wanted to draw the curtains.*

Why are tall people always the laziest?
> *Because they lie longest in bed.*

Why does a man never go thirsty in the desert with a watch?
> *Because every watch has a spring.*

Why did a man throw his watch out of the window?
> *To see time fly.*

Why does lightning shock people?
> *It doesn't know how to conduct itself.*

Why is the theatre such a sad place?
> *The seats are always in tiers.*

Why did the cleaning woman stop cleaning?
Because she found grime doesn't pay.

Why did the thief take a bath?
So he could make a clean getaway.

Why do they put telephone wires so high?
To keep up the conversation.

Why is a radio never complete?
It's always a wireless.

Why is a newspaper like an army?
It has leaders, columns and reviewers.

Who invented vulgar fractions?
Henry the $\frac{1}{8}$.

Who invented the first fireplace?
Alfred the Grate.

Who invented fire?
Oh, some bright spark.

Who invented the five day week?
Robinson Crusoe. He had all his work done by Friday.

Who gets the sack every time he goes to work?
The postman.

Who was the world's first underwater spy?
James Pond.

Where did Hitler keep his armies?
Up his sleevies.

Who invented gunpowder?
A woman who wanted guns to look pretty.

Where would a man post a letter in his sleep?
In a pillow-box.

Where do elves go to get fit?
Elf farms.

Which is the fastest, heat or cold?
Heat, because you can catch cold.

How does a fireplace feel when you fill it with coal?
Grate-full.

How many weeks belong to a year?
Forty-six. The other six are only Lent.

How does an intruder get into the house?
Intruder window.

JUDY: 'Do you believe in free speech?'
PUNCH: 'I certainly do.'
JUDY: 'Good, can I use your telephone?'

Do mountains have ears?
Yes, they have mountaineers.

38

'Did you know that Davy Crockett had three ears?'
'No, how was that?'
'He had a right ear, a left ear, and a wild frontier.'

Can you name three inventions that have helped man to get up in the world?
The elevator, the escalator, and the alarm clock.

A barrel of beer fell on a man. Why wasn't he hurt?
It was light ale.

Shall I tell you the joke about the pencil?
No, there's no point in it.

Shall I tell you the joke about the bed?
No, it hasn't been made yet.

Hickory dickory dock
Three mice ran up the clock
The clock struck one . . .
and the other two got away with minor injuries!

CINEMA ATTENDANT: 'That's the sixth ticket you've bought.'

CUSTOMER: 'Yes, I know, there's a girl in there that keeps tearing them up.'

WOMAN: 'I bought a carpet which was in mint condition.'

NEIGHBOUR: 'What do you mean?'

WOMAN: 'There was a hole in the middle.'

MAN: 'You've been working in your garden for hours. What are you growing?'

GARDENER: 'Tired.'

COLIN: 'You remind me of the sea.'

ANN: 'Because I'm so wild, reckless and romantic?'

COLIN: 'No, you make me sick.'

AUNT: 'Dick, why are you scratching yourself?'

DICK: 'No one else knows where I itch.'

MAN: 'I say, what's that bad cut doing on your forehead?'

NUT: 'I bit myself.'

MAN: 'But how did you get up there?'

NUT: 'I stood on a chair.'

JUDGE: 'Have you been up before me before?'

THIEF: 'I don't know, what time do you get up?'

'Mummy, does God use our bathroom?'

'No darling, why?'

'Because every morning Daddy bangs on the door and shouts, "Oh God, are you still in there?"'

'My brother gets a warm reception wherever he goes.'

'He must be very popular.'

'No, he's a fireman.'

The vacancy is for a litter-collector. Have you any experience?

> *No, but I'll pick it up as I go along.*

Have you heard the one about the man who bought a paper shop?

> *It blew away.*

Have you heard the one about the man who always wore sunglasses?

> *He took a dim view of things.*

Have you heard the one about the boy who stood in front of the mirror with his eyes closed?

'Why are you doing that?' asked his sister.

'To see what I look like when I am asleep,' replied the boy.

I have five noses, six mouths and seven ears. What am I?

> *Quite ugly.*

Think of a number between one and fifty. Double it, subtract sixty-one, add one, subtract the number you started with, close your eyes . . .

> *Dark isn't it!*

Keep smiling. It makes everybody wonder what you're up to.

'THERE WAS A YOUNG FELLOW...'

FIVE FRIVOLOUS LIMERICKS

THERE WAS A YOUNG LADY
NAMED PERKINS...

A BANDY-LEGGED POLICEMAN FROM KEW...

There was a young
lady from Gloucester...

THERE WAS A YOUNG BARD
from JAPAN...

there once were a couple
of llamas...

There was a young lady named Perkins,
Who was very fond of small gherkins.
  One day at tea
  She ate forty-three,
And pickled her internal workings.

      A bandy-legged policeman from Kew
      Said, 'I really don't know what to do.
        I can stop without fuss
        A lorry or bus,
      But bubble cars simply go through.'

There was a young lady from Gloucester,
Whose parents thought they had lost her.
  From the fridge came a sound
  And at last she was found.
The trouble was – how to defrost her.

      There was a young bard from Japan,
      Whose limericks never would scan.
        When they said it was so,
        He replied, 'Yes, I know,
      But I make a rule of always trying to get just as many words into the last line as I possibly can.'

There once were a couple of llamas,
Who swaggered in silken pyjamas,
　　But in coldest of weathers
　　They wished they wore feathers
Like Orpingtons, Dorkings or Brahmas.

　　　　A jolly old bear at the zoo
　　　　Could always find something to do.
　　　　　　When it bored him to go
　　　　　　On a walk to and fro,
　　　　He reversed it and walked fro and to.

A girl who weighed many an oz.
Used language I dare not pron. oz.
　　For a fellow unkind
　　Pulled her chair out behind,
Just to see (so he said) if she'd bounce.

mutts and mousers

what's an octupus?

WHAT GOES WUFF, WUFF, TICK, TICK?

what's a cat's favourite holiday resort?

what are blue-blooded, short legged and live in a palace?

It's raining cats and dogs!?

WHAT HAPPENED TO THE CAT WHO SWALLOWED A BALL OF WOOL?

What do you get when you cross a jelly with a sheep dog?
Collie-wobbles.

What happened to the cat who swallowed a ball of wool?
She had mittens.

What is an octopus?
An eight-sided cat.

WILLIE: 'It's raining cats and dogs today.'
BOB: 'I know – I've just stepped into a poodle.'

'Daddy, there's a black cat in the dining-room.'
'But son, black cats are lucky.'
'This one is – he's eaten your dinner.'

Why is it that every time the doorbell rings, my dog goes into a corner?
He's a boxer.

What noise does a cat make going down the M1?
Miaooooooooooooooooooooow!

'I've lost my dog.'
'Why don't you put an advertisement in the paper?'
'Don't be silly – he can't read.'

How does a dog make friends?
He wags his tail instead of his tongue.

What do you call a very small cat that joins the St John Ambulance Brigade?
A first-aid kit.

Why does a dog chase its tail?
To make both ends meet.

BULLDOG FOR SALE.
Will eat anything – very fond of children.

What cat is best in the library?
A catalogue.

What's the difference between a dog and a flea?
> *The dog can have a flea but the flea can't have a dog.*

What goes 'wuff, wuff, tick, tick'?
> *A watchdog.*

What do we call a cat who has
swallowed a duck?
> *A 'duck-filled-fatty-puss'.*

What do cats strive for?
> *Purrfection.*

What do you call a cat that
sucks acid drops?
> *A sour puss.*

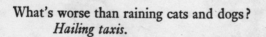

What's a cat's favourite
holiday resort?
> *The Canary Islands.*

What's worse than raining cats and dogs?
> *Hailing taxis.*

When is a brown dog not a brown dog?
> *When it's a greyhound.*

When is it bad luck to have a black cat follow you?
> *When you are a mouse.*

What book was written by a cat?
> *The Thoughts of Meou Tse Tung.*

FIRST CLEVER DICK: 'Every day my dog and I go for a tramp in the woods.'
SECOND CLEVER DICK: 'Does the dog enjoy it?'
FIRST CLEVER DICK: 'Yes, but the tramp's getting a bit fed up.'

What are blue-blooded, short-legged, and live in a palace?
The Queen's corgi dogs.

What did the cowboy say to his dog when it fell off the cliff?
Dawg gone.

When should a mouse carry an umbrella?
When it's raining cats and dogs.

Nosh-up

WHY ARE COOKS CRUEL?

How do you make a sausage roll?

when are the streets most greasy?

"WAITER, WAITER, WILL THE PANCAKES BE LONG?"

what did the traffic warden have in his sandwiches?

What's the fastest thing in the world?
>   *Milk – because it's past your eyes before you see it.*

Why are cooks cruel?
>   *They beat eggs, whip cream and batter fish.*

Two ears of corn ran up a hill. What were they when they got to the top?
>   *Puffed wheat.*

Did you hear about the man who stole some rhubarb?
>   *He was put into custardy.*

What did the traffic warden have in his sandwiches?
>   *Traffic jam.*

What do jelly-babies wear on their feet?
>   *Gum-boots.*

RICH CUSTOMER ON PHONE TO FISHMONGER:
'Please deliver me a dozen oysters, not too large, not too small, not very old, not tough and not sandy.'
FISHMONGER: 'Certainly, madam. With or without pearls?'

What happened to the man who couldn't tell putty from porridge?
>   *His windows fell out.*

What cake is dangerous?
Attila the Bun.

What's yellow and stupid?
Thick custard.

What did Adam do when he wanted sugar?
He raised Cain.

A girl in a sweetshop is one metre, fifty centimetres tall, and wears size four shoes. What does she weigh?
Sweets.

What's a frog's favourite sweet?
A lollihop.

What's huge, icy and tastes delicious?
A glacier mint.

When is a red-headed idiot like a biscuit?
When he's a ginger nut.

What's a lawyer's favourite pudding?
Sue-it.

What do the Bay City Rollers have for dinner?
Tartan Custard.

What do pixies have for tea?
Fairy cakes.

Why did the cookie cry?
Because its mother had been a wafer so long.

What tree has the best food?
A pantry.

Why did the baker stop making doughnuts?
>*Because he got tired of the hole business.*

What's white and fluffy and beats its chest in a cake shop?
>*A meringue-utang.*

What did the mayonnaise say to the fridge?
>*Close the door, I'm dressing.*

Do you know the joke about the cornflakes and the shredded wheat who had a fight?
>*I can only tell you a little, as it's a serial.*

A door-to-door salesman knocked on the door.
SALESMAN: 'Would you like to try our new oatmeal soap?'
MAN: 'No thanks, I never wash my oatmeal.'

What can you put in the fridge that will stay hot?
>*Mustard.*

How do you know a sausage doesn't like being fried?
>*Because it spits.*

How do you make a sausage roll?
>*Push it.*

TEACHER: 'In some countries they use fish as a medium of exchange.'
TOMMY: 'Gosh, it must be a messy business getting chocolate out of a machine.'

What did the hamburger say to the tomato?
That's enough of your sauce.

There was a polite family having dinner. Their little girl asked if she could leave the table and her little brother answered: 'She can't really take it with her can she?'

MOTHER: 'Now, Sally, don't you know you are not supposed to eat with your knife?'
SALLY: 'Yes, Mother, but my fork leaks.'

Should you stir your tea with your left hand or right?
Neither. You should stir it with a spoon.

What's the difference between a nightwatchman and a butcher?
One stays awake and the other weighs a steak.

WOMAN: 'I want four nice pork chops please, and make them lean.'
BUTCHER: 'Certainly, madam, which way?'

Two eggs in a pan. One said: 'It's hot in here, isn't it?'
The other one said: 'Wait until you get out, you have your head bashed in.'

'Have you heard the joke about the eggs?'
'No.'
'Two bad.'

What goes 100 m.p.h. on the railway lines and is yellow and white?

A train-driver's egg sandwich.

LADY: 'I found a fly in one of those currant buns you sold me yesterday.'

SHOP ASSISTANT: 'Well, bring the fly back and I'll exchange it for a currant.'

How can you stop food going bad?

Eat it.

What would you call five bottles of lemonade?

A pop group.

What's very tall and stands in the middle of Paris, wobbling like a jelly?

The Trifle Tower.

When are the streets most greasy?

When the rain is dripping.

What grows in gardens, makes a sandwich, and is dangerous if you run into it?

A hambush.

PARSON: 'Do you say your prayers before dinner, Andrew?'
ANDREW: 'No sir, my Mum's a good cook.'

DINER: 'This restaurant must have a very clean kitchen.'
OWNER: 'Thank you, sir, but how did you know?'
DINER: 'Everything tastes of soap.'

'Waiter, waiter, will the pancakes be long?'
       'No, sir, round.'

'Waiter, what soup is this?'
'It's bean soup, sir.'
'I don't care what it was, I want to know what it is now.'

'Waiter, waiter, there's a fly in my soup!'
       'Don't worry, sir, the spider in the salad will get it.'

DINER: 'I say, waiter. There's a twig in my soup.'
WAITER: 'Hold on, sir, I'll call the branch manager.'

DINER: 'What's wrong with these eggs?'
WAITER: 'Don't ask me, sir. I only laid the table.'

DINER: 'Why has this lobster only got one claw?'
WAITER: 'I think it must have been in a fight, sir.'
DINER: 'Well, maybe you could bring me the winner.'

'Waiter, waiter, there's a fly in my soup.'
       'Don't tell everyone or they'll all want one.'

MAN IN A RESTAURANT: 'Waiter, there's a dead fly in my
   soup!'
WAITER: 'Yes, sir, it's the hot water that kills them.'

'Waiter, there's a fly in my soup.'
       'If you hold on a minute, sir, I'll fetch the R.S.P.C.A.'

59

'Waiter, waiter, have you got frogs' legs?'
   'No, sir, I always walk this way.'

'Waiter, waiter, have you got frogs' legs?'
'Certainly, sir.'
'Then leap over the counter and get me a drink.'

'Waiter, do you serve crabs?'
   'Sit down, sir, we serve anybody.'

WAITER: 'How did you find your steak, sir?'
DINER: 'Quite by accident. I moved a few peas and there
   it was.'

'Waiter, this coffee tastes like earth!'
   'I'm not surprised, it was ground this morning.'

TELLY WHO?

what's yellow and sings?

WHAT'S PURPLE AND FLIES IN OUTER SPACE?

what kind of pen does Kojak use?

WHAT SWINGS ABOUT A CAKE SHOP YODELLING?

what do you use to measure a tartan?

What's Yellow and sings?
  (*Ba*)*Nana Mouskouri.*

What do you call a lazy Stegosaurus?
  A Stegosnaurus.

What's purple and flies in outer space?
  Planet of the grapes.

What lives in pods and is a Kung Fu expert?
  Bruce Pea.

What swings about a cake-shop yodelling?
  Tarzipan.

What do you get if you cross Larry Grayson, an Indian and Tommy Cooper?
  Everard, shut that door. How? Just like that.

The bionic man was stopped at 115 m.p.h. on the M6 – he was fined £15 and dismantled for 6 months.

Did you hear about the man who thought the Rover 3500 was a bionic dog?

What washing powder does Kojak use?
Bald Automatic.

What is Kojak's hobby?
Watching Telly.

What kind of pen does Kojak use?
A baldpoint pen.

What did Kojak say to Ironside?
Who shoves you, baby?

Two flies on Kojak's head. One fly said to the other,
'Smile,' and the other one said, 'Why?'
And the first fly said, 'We're on Telly.'

Why did Kojak throw away his keys?
Because he didn't have any locks.

Why will television never take the place of newspapers?
Have you ever tried swatting a fly with a television?

What's blue and flies through the trees?
Tarzan in a boiler suit.

Why should Basil Brush be in a football team?
Because he would make a very good sweeper.

What were Tarzan's last words?
　　Who greased that vine?

'What's on the television tonight, son?'
'Same as usual, dad, the goldfish bowl and lamp.'

A ZOO LIKE IT

What keys are furry?

What lion never moves?

WHAT'S A CROCODILE'S FAVOURITE GAME?

How do you keep a skunk from smelling?

WHY IS IT DANGEROUS TO PLAY CARDS IN THE JUNGLE?

What's the biggest species of mouse in the world?
The hippopotamouse.

What weighs two thousand pounds and wears a flower behind its ear?
A hippy potamus.

What's green and slimy and goes hith?
A snake with a lisp.

What's yellow and black with red spots?
A leopard with measles.

What's black and white and noisy?
A zebra with a set of drums.

What's white, furry, and smells of peppermint?
A polo bear.

What did the Polar bear have for lunch?
Ice burgers.

What animal do you eat for pudding?
A moose.

What keys are furry?
Monkeys.

What lion never moves?
A dandelion.

What are the best steps to take when you meet an escaped lion?
Very long ones.

What's the difference between a lion with a toothache and a rainstorm?
One roars with pain and the other pours with rain.

What do you call a gorilla with a tommy-gun?
Sir.

What do gorillas sing at Christmastime?
'Jungle bells, Jungle bells.'

What did the skunk say when the wind changed direction?
'Ah, it's all coming back to me now.'

What runs around forests making other animals yawn?
A wild bore.

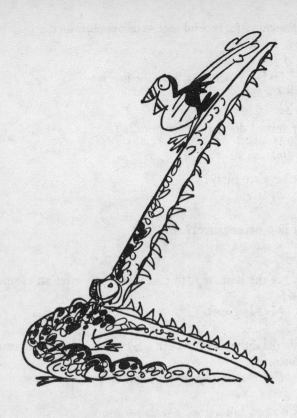

What's a crocodile's favourite game?
Snap.

What do you get if you cross a crocodile with a rose?
I don't know, but I wouldn't try smelling it.

What do you get if you cross a zebra with a pig?
Striped sausages.

What do you get if you cross a giraffe with a dog?
An animal that barks at low-flying aircraft.

What animals has two humps and is found at the North Pole?

    A lost camel.

What did the traffic light say to the zebra crossing?

    'Don't look now, I'm changing.'

How do you keep a skunk from smelling?

    Hold his nose.

Why do leopards never escape from the zoo?
Because they're always spotted.

Why did the elephant cross the road?
Because it was the chicken's day off.

A lion was walking through the jungle when he came across a deer eating grass in a clearing. The lion roared, 'Who is the King of the jungle?' and the deer replied, 'Oh, you are, Master.' The lion walked off pleased. Soon he came across a zebra drinking at a water hole. The lion roared, 'Who is the King of the jungle?' and the zebra replied, 'Oh, you are, Master.' The lion walked off pleased. Then he came across an elephant. 'Who is the King of the jungle?' he roared. With that the elephant threw the lion across a tree and jumped on him. The lion scraped himself up off the ground and said, 'Okay, okay, there's no need to get mad just because you don't know the answer.'

Why is it dangerous to play cards in the jungle?
Because there are so many cheetahs.

SHOW-OFF: ' . . . so I just leapt out of bed, grabbed my gun and shot the tiger in my pyjamas.'
CLEVER DICK: 'Goodness me, what was a tiger doing in your pyjamas?'

There are two snakes in a jungle. One snake says to the other, 'Are we supposed to be poisonous?' and the other snake says, 'Why?'
'Because I have just bitten my lip,' says the first snake.

ANNIE
WHO?

KNOCK. KNOCK,
who's there?

ANNIE

Annie who?

ANNIVERSARY

What did the jack say to the car?
Can I give you a lift?

What do you call a three-wheeler convertible with a double exhaust pipe?
A wheelbarrow.

What do you call a three-wheeler with a football in the front seat?
A whistle.

What do you get if you cross a centipede with a parrot?
A walkie-talkie.

A story
Once there was a man who couldn't get a job anywhere. He had been out of work for years. He'd been on all the courses. He'd been to all the job interviews. There was only one job left – a job at the zoo. So the next morning he went down to the zoo and asked the keeper if he had any jobs spare.

'I'm sorry, we haven't ... Oh, actually I think we have. All our monkeys have run away. Could you dress up as a monkey for me?'

'Yes, certainly,' the man replied (as he was desperate for a job). So he put on the monkey suit and got into a cage right next door to the lions.

It wasn't too long before he noticed a large hole in the wire between his cage and the lions'. Then one of the lions noticed the hole in the wire too, and ambled through into the monkey cage.

The man in the monkey suit started shouting out, 'Oh please, pleeease, pleeeease don't eat me. I'm not a monkey, I'm a person. And I'm a very skinny person!'

And the lion replied: 'Shut up! Keep your voice down or we'll all be out of a job.'

What's green, curved and goes slam, slam, slam?
A cucumber hatchback.

What do you get when you cross a cow, a sheep and a young goat?
The milky baa kid.

'Doctor! Doctor! Everyone keeps ignoring me!'
'Next please!'

Why did Little Bo Peep lose her sheep?
She had a crook with her.

SON: Dad, I don't need a bike for Christmas any more.
DAD: Why not?
SON: I found one behind the wardrobe.

What spins and does not stop?
The world.

Why did Frank Carson tell jokes to the eggs?
'Cos he wanted to crack them up.

What happens to tyres when they get old?
They get retired.

What happens to bikes when they get old?
They get recycled.

What do you call someone who speaks three languages?
>*Tri-lingual.*

What do you call someone who speaks two languages?
>*Bi-lingual.*

What do you call someone who speaks one language?
>*English.*

Who was the first person to wear a shell suit?
>*Humpty Dumpty.*

What did the dentist say when she saw something bad?
>*Oh, sugar!!*

If I had 50p in one pocket and 25p in the other pocket, what would I have?
>*Someone else's trousers.*

What's yellow, brown and hairy?
>*Cheese and toast on the carpet*

What happened to the girl who slept under the pillow?
>*The tooth fairy took her head away.*

There was a young monster called Fred
Who always ate garlic in bed.
His mother said, 'Son,
That's really not done!
Why don't you eat humans instead?'

Why doesn't Cinderella play football well?
>*Because she had a pumpkin for a coach.*

'Waiter, waiter! There's a footprint in my pudding!'
>*'Well, sir, you did tell me to step on it.'*

What's the difference between a camera and a sock?
> *You put five toes in a sock, and photos (four toes) in a camera.*

What does the invisible man call his mum and dad?
> *Transparents.*

Why did the frog jump into the pond when it began to rain?
> *To stop getting wet.*

How can you drop a pizza ten feet without it breaking?
> *Drop it eleven feet, and for the first ten feet it will remain as a pizza.*

There were two boys called Jim and Bill in the same class. They'd had a test, and the teacher called Bill out to her desk, and said:

'Have you been copying your work, Bill?'

'No, Miss,' said Bill.

'But for the first answer Jim put "Yes" and you put "Yes" . . .'

'So what, Miss!' said Bill.

'. . . and for the second answer Jim put "I don't know" and you put "Neither do I".'

'Um, Miss . . .'

What is big and red and eats rocks?
> *A big red rock eater.*

What did the launch pad say to the rocket?
> *Clear off. You're fired.*

Where can you always find a cow?
> *In a mooseum.*

Henry and Sid were walking across the road, and Sid fell down a manhole. Henry shouted down to Sid, 'Is it dark down there?' Sid called back, 'Dunno. I can't see anything.'

'Why doesn't the Queen wave with this hand?' (Hold up your left hand.)
  'I don't know.'
  'Because it's my hand, not the Queen's hand.'

MARVIN: How much are those puppies in the window?
SHOPKEEPER: Thirty pounds apiece.
MARVIN: OK. But how much is a whole one?

What's the name of the song when fish sing, 'Bedtime, Bedtime'?
> *Salmon chanted evening.*

What did Pink Panther say when he stood on an ant?
> *Dead ant. Dead ant. Dead ant dead ant dead ant . . .*

What's black and white and black and white and black and white?
> *A puffin rolling downhill.*

And what's black and white and laughing?
> *The second puffin who pushed the first one down the hill.*

RIB TICKLERS

WHAT JOBS
DO HIPPIES
DO?

what do
snowmen
dance at?

what game does
the wind play?

WHAT DID ONE LIFT SAY TO
THE OTHER LIFT?

what runs but nerer moves?
what runs with
its head
down?

What did the gas meter say to the five-pence piece?
Glad you dropped in, I was just going out.

What did the big chimney say to the little chimney?
You're too young to smoke.

What did the chimney-sweep say when he was asked if he liked his work?
It soots me.

What did the coke say to the coal?
What kind of fuel am I?

What did the big fire-cracker say to the little fire-cracker?
My pop is bigger than yours.

What did the bell say when it fell in the water?
I'm wringing wet.

What did Hamlet say when he went into a telephone box?
2p or not 2p, that is the question.

What jobs do hippies do?
They hold your leggies on.

What do you feed under-nourished dwarfs?
Elf-raising flour.

What did they do when the Forth Bridge collapsed?
Built a fifth.

What did one lift say to the other lift?
I think I'm going down with something.

What did the electrician's wife say when he arrived home late?
Wire you insulate?

What did the south wind say to the north wind?
Let's play draughts.

What has a neck but cannot swallow?
A bottle.

What never asks questions but gets plenty of answers?
A doorbell.

What part of the army could a baby join?
The infantry.

What do snowmen dance at?
A snowball.

What runs but never moves?
A fence.

What's white and dashes through the desert with a bed-pan?
Florence of Arabia.

What's the most shocking city in the world?
Electri-city.

What always walks with its head down?
    A nail in your shoe.

What goes up and down but never moves?
    Stairs.

What kind of bow is impossible to tie?
    A rainbow.

What gets lost every time you stand up?
    Your lap.

What sort of robbery is the easiest?
    A safe robbery.

What did the burglar say to the lady of the house when she
    caught him stealing her silver?
        '*I am at your service, Ma'am.*'

What did the burglar say to the watchmaker?
        '*Sorry to have taken so much of your valuable time.*'

What prize did the man who invented doorknockers win?
    The Nobel Prize.

What is a good name for the wife of an engineer?
> *Bridget.*

What man claps at Christmas?
> *Santaplause.*

What sort of woman can get a man to give her the shirt off his back?
> *A laundress.*

What's higher than an admiral?
> *His hat.*

What is always coming but never arrives?
> *Tomorrow.*

What's the best thing to give as a parting gift?
> *A comb.*

What grows bigger the more you take from it?
> *A hole.*

What is a blooming nuisance?
> *A weed.*

What can go up a drainpipe down, but can't go down a drainpipe up?
> *An umbrella.*

What's the only business you can see through?
> *Window-cleaning.*

What does the sea say to the sand?
> *Nothing, it just waves.*

What can fall on water without getting wet?
A shadow.

What would you do if you swallowed a light bulb?
Use a candle.

What's got teeth but can't bite?
A comb.

What's the best system of book-keeping?
Never lend them.

What's the best way to keep water out of the house?
Don't pay the water rates.

What do you call a Scottish cloakroom-attendant?
Angus McCoatup.

What do you call a building with lots of storeys?
A library.

What is frozen water? Ice.
What is frozen cream? Ice cream.
What is frozen tea? Iced tea.
What is frozen ink? Iced ink.
Well, have a bath then!

What's the last thing you take off before you go to bed?
Your feet off the floor.

What's the difference between a sailor and a bargain shopper?
One goes to sail the seas, the other to see the sales.

What's the difference between a plane and a tree?
One leaves its shed and the other sheds its leaves.

What's the difference between a postage stamp and a girl?
One is a mail fee and the other a female.

What's the difference between a thief and a church bell?
> *One steals from the people and the other peals from the steeple.*

What's the cure for water on the brain?
> *A tap on the head.*

What's the difference between a mad king and a street?
> *One tosses crowns and the other crosses towns.*

What's the difference between a sigh, a motor car and a monkey?
> *A sigh is oh dear.*
> *A car is too dear.*
> *A monkey is you, dear.*

Hoarse Laughs

WHERE DO YOU TAKE A SICK HORSE?

what horse can't you ride?

What exams do horses take?

Can you spell a hungry horse in four letters?

Where do you take a sick horse?
Horsepital.

Why did the jockey take his hay to bed?
To feed his nightmares.

What always goes to bed with his shoes on?
A horse.

What game do horses like playing best?
Stable tennis.

What horse can't you ride?
A clothes horse.

What do you give a pony with a cold?
Cough stirrup.

What exams do horses take?
Hay levels.

Spell a hungry horse in four letters.
M.T.G.G.

RONNIE: 'Is your new hunting horse well behaved?'
JOHNNIE: 'He certainly is! He has such good manners
   that when we came to a fence he stopped and let me go
   first.'

What is horse sense?
Just stable thinking.

WILLY: 'I found a horseshoe today. What do you think it
   means?'
SILLY: 'Perhaps the horse decided to wear socks instead.'

KNOCK-KNOCK
"who's there?"
-Atch.
Atch who?
-Ana.
Ana who?
-IVOR.
IVOR WHO?
-alec.
alec who?
-NOISE.
NOISE WHO?
-KEN.
KEN WHO?

Knock, knock.
Who's there?
Amos.
Amos who?
A mosquito.

Knock, knock.
Who's there?
Arthur.
Arthur who?
Arthur any more biscuits
   in the larder?

Knock, knock.
Who's there?
Luke.
Luke who?
Luke through the
   keyhole and you'll see.

Knock, knock.
Who's there?
Lettuce.
Lettuce who?
Lettuce in and you'll
   find out.

Knock, knock.
Who's there?
Anna.
Anna who?
Another mosquito.

Knock, knock.
Who's there?
Atch.
Atch who?
Sorry, I didn't know you
   had a cold.

Knock, knock.
Who's there?
Wilma.
Wilma who?
Wilma supper be ready
   soon?

Knock, knock.
Who's there?
Tick.
Tick who?
Tick 'em up, I'm a
   tongue-tied cowboy.

Knock, knock.
Who's there?
Egbut.
Egbut who?
Egbut no bacon.

Knock, knock.
Who's there?
Tish.
Tish who?
Tishoo.

Knock, knock.
Who's there?
Walter.
Walter who?
Walter wall carpets.

Knock, knock.
Who's there?
Ivor.
Ivor who?
Ivor you let me in the door or I'll climb in the window.

Knock, knock.
Who's there?
Arfer.
Arfer who?
Arfer got.

Knock, knock.
Who's there?
William.
William who?
Williamind your own business.

Knock, knock.
Who's there?
Olive.
Olive who?
Olive here, so let me in!

Knock, knock.
Who's there?
Sarah.
Sarah who?
Sarah a doctor in the house?

KNOCK KNOCK!

Knock, knock.
Who's there?
Dismay.
Dismay who?
Dismay be a joke but
  it doesn't make me
  laugh.

Knock, knock.
Who's there?
Toby.
Toby who?
Toby or not Toby, that
  is the question.

Knock, knock.
Who's there?
Ken.
Ken who?
Ken I come in?

Knock, knock.
Who's there?
Shirley.
Shirley who?
Shirley I don't need to
  tell you!

Knock, knock.
Who's there?
Alison.
Alison who?
Alison to my radio.

Knock, knock.
Who's there?
Cook.
Cook who?
That's the first one
  I've heard this year.

Knock, knock.
Who's there?
Kanga.
Kanga who?
No, Kangaroo.

Knock, knock.
Who's there?
Amy.
Amy who?
Amy fraid I've forgotten.

Knock, knock.
Who's there?
Watson.
Watson who?
Watson television?

Knock, knock.
Who's there?
Ginger.
Ginger who?
Ginger fall off the wall?

Knock, knock.
Who's there?
Isabel.
Isabel who?
Isabel really necessary on
 a bike?

Knock, knock.
Who's there?
Frank.
Frank who?
Frankly, I don't know.

Knock, knock.
Who's there?
Hugo.
Hugo who?
Hugo that way and I'll
 go this way.

Knock, knock.
Who's there?
Alec.
Alec who?
Alec a nice cup of tea in
 the morning.

Knock, knock.
Who's there?
Scot.
Scot who?
Scot nothing to do with
 you.

Knock, knock.
Who's there?
Granny.
Knock, knock.
Who's there?
Granny.
Knock, knock.
Who's there?
Granny.
Knock, knock.
Who's there?
Aunt.
Aunt who?
Aunt you glad I got rid
 of all those grannies?

Knock, knock.
Who's there?
Madam.
Madam who?
Ma damn fist's stuck in
 the door.

Knock, knock.
Who's there?
Noise.
Noise who?
Noise to see yer.

Knock, knock.
Who's there?
Martini.
Martini who?
Martini hands are frozen.

Knock, knock.
Who's there?
Author.
Author who?
Author any more at
     home like you?

Knock, knock.
Who's there?
Irish stew.
Irish stew who?
Irish stew in the name
     of the law!

Knock, knock.
Who's there?
Cows go.
Cows go who?
Cows go moo not who.

Knock, knock.
Who's there?
You.
You who?
Did you call?

Knock, knock.
Who's there?
A little old lady.
A little old lady who?
I didn't know you
     could yodel.

Knock, knock.
Who's there?
A man who can't reach
     the doorbell.

Will you remember me in a month?
      Of course.
Will you remember me in a year?
      Certainly.
Will you remember me in two years?
      Yes.
Will you remember me in three years?
      Of course!
Knock, knock.
      Who's there?
See, you've forgotten me already.

School Rulers
Did you hear about the teacher who was cross-eyed?
HOW CAN YOU PROVE THE WORLD IS ROUND?
HOW DO YOU SPELL 'CROCODILE'?
Did your Big brother help you with your homework?

FRED: 'Dad, I'm too tired to do my homework.'
DAD: 'Now my lad, hard work never killed anyone yet.'
FRED: 'So why should I run the risk of being the first?'

Why did the teacher wear dark glasses?
Because the class was so bright.

Did you hear about the teacher who was cross-eyed?
She couldn't control her pupils.

'How do you spell "Crocodile"?'
"K-r-o-k-o-d-i-a-l."
'The dictionary spells it "C-r-o-c-o-d-i-l-e".'
'You didn't ask me how the dictionary spelt it.'

What's the difference between a fisherman and a bad boy
  at school?
One baits his hooks and the other hates his books.

TEACHER: 'Name four animals of the cat family.'
PUPIL: 'Father cat, Mother cat, and two kittens.'

A little girl opened the door to her teacher.
  'Are your parents in?' asked the teacher.
  'They was in,' said the little girl, 'but they is out now.'
  'They WAS in! They IS out!' exclaimed the teacher.
    'Where is your grammar?'
  'In the front room watching the telly.'

FATHER: 'Well, Johnny, do you think the teacher likes you?'
JOHNNY: 'Oh yes, she puts a wee kiss by all my sums.'

SALLY: 'Would you punish a pupil for something she didn't do?'
TEACHER: 'Of course not.'
SALLY: 'Good, I haven't done my homework.'

TEACHER: 'Now Damion, you shouldn't fight, you should learn to give and take.'
DAMION: 'I did, I gave him a black eye and took his orange.'

TEACHER: 'Andy, say something beginning with "I".'
ANDY: 'I is . . .'
TEACHER: 'No, Andy, you must say I am.'
ANDY: 'All right, I am the ninth letter of the alphabet.'

TEACHER: 'If I had forty apples in one hand and fifty in the other, what would I have?'
TOMMY: 'Big hands.'

TEACHER: 'I wish you'd pay a little attention.'
PUPIL: I'm paying as little as I can.'

TEACHER: 'Johnson, stop showing off. Do you think you're the teacher of this class?'
BOY: 'No, sir.'
TEACHER: 'Right, then stop behaving like a fool.'

TEACHER: 'Where is your pencil, Tommy?'
TOMMY: 'I ain't got one.'
TEACHER: 'Not "ain't" – "haven't". I haven't got my pencil, you haven't got a pencil, they haven't got pencils.'
TOMMY: 'Gee! What happened to all the pencils?'

TEACHER: 'Where are the Andes?'
THE NEW BOY: 'At the end of my armies.'

TEACHER (on phone): 'You say Jimmy has a cold and can't come to school? To whom am I speaking?'
VOICE: 'This is my father.'

TEACHER: 'Johnny, how can you prove the world is round?'
JOHNNY: 'I never said it was, miss.'

TEACHER: 'Did your big brother help you with your home-work, Harry?'
HARRY: 'No, miss, he did all the work himself.'

TEACHER TO SMALL BOY: 'You should have been here at nine o'clock.'
BOY: 'Why, what happened?'

ANGRY MAN: 'I'll teach you to throw stones at my green-house.'
SCHOOLBOY: 'I wish you would. I've had ten shots and haven't hit it yet.'

TEACHER: 'Give me a sentence with the word "centi-metre" in it, Jimmy.'
JIMMY: 'Er ... My aunt was coming home from the country and I was centimetre.'

TEACHER: 'Take this sentence, "Let the cow be taken to the pasture." Now, what mood?'
JIMMY: 'The cow, sir?'

FIRST STUDENT: 'How were your exam questions?'
SECOND STUDENT: 'They were easy, but I had trouble with the answers.'

TEACHER: 'If we breathe oxygen in the daytime, what do we breathe at night?'
GRACIE: 'Nitrogen?'

MOTHER TO SON: 'Come on, you'll be late for school.'
'Shan't,' came the reply from the bedroom.
'Why, what's wrong?'
'The teachers hate me and the kids despise me.'
'I'll give you two good reasons why you should go.'
'What are they?'
'One – you're forty-one, and two – you're the headmaster.'

An orange went to telephone a friend but the other orange didn't give her the message. Why?

Because the pips went.

What's purple and hums?

An electric plum.

What's yellow and goes 'slam, slam, slam, slam'?

A four-door banana.

What's a good way of putting on weight?

Eat a peach, swallow the centre, and you've gained a stone.

What sits in a fruit bowl and shouts for help?

A damson in distress.

What do you give a hurt lemon?

Give it lemonade, of course.

How do you make an apple puff?

Chase it round the garden.

What's orange and comes out of the ground at 100 m.p.h.?

A jet-propelled carrot.

What vegetable should you pick to go with jacket potatoes?

Button mushrooms.

What's the difference between a mouldy lettuce and a dismal song?

One's bad salad and the other's a sad ballad.

What's yellow on the inside and green on the outside?

A banana disguised as a cucumber.

What do you do if you find a blue banana?

Try to cheer it up.

What room has no floor or ceiling, windows or doors?

A mushroom.

What's green and goes 'boing, boing, boing'?

A spring cabbage.

What are two rows of cabbages called?

A dual cabbage-way.

What vegetable needs a plumber?

A leek.

What stands on one leg and has its heart in its head?
A cabbage.

What letter is a vegetable?
A P.

What's green and holds up stage-coaches?
Dick Gherkin.

What is the fastest vegetable?
A runner bean.

Why don't you tell secrets in vegetable gardens?
Because corn has ears and beans talk.

Why is history the sweetest lesson?
Because it's full of dates.

Why wouldn't the man eat an apple?
His grandmother died of apple-plexy.

Why is the apple-tree crying?
Because people are always picking at him.

How can you tell that coconut juice is nutty?
Because it lives in a padded cell.

How do you calculate the colour of plums?
Use a green gauge.

How do you make gold soup?
Put fourteen carrots in it.

Woman in a greengrocer's: 'One pound of mixed nuts and not too many coconuts, please.'

Dumb Clucks

WHICH BIRDS ARE RELIGIOUS?

WHY DO BIRDS FLY SOUTH IN WINTER?

what always grows up while it grows down?

WHAT IS A BIRD AFTER ITS 4 DAYS OLD?

what letter is a bird?

On which side does a chicken have most feathers?
On the outside.

Which bird can lift the heaviest weights?
The crane.

Which birds are religious?
Birds of prey.

What letter is a bird?
A J.

What pies can fly?

Magpies.

What would a baby goose say if it saw an orange in its nest?
'Look at the orange marmalade.'

What is a parrot stuffed with?
Polyfilla.

What kind of bird do you find down a coal-pit?
A mynah bird.

What kind of bird is like a car?
A goose is like a car, because they both go honk.

What is a bird after he is four days old?
Five days old.

What do birds eat for their breakfast?
Tweet-a-bix and shredded tweet.

What always succeeds?
A budgie with no teeth.

What grows up while
it grows down?
A baby duckling.

What do you get when you cross a carrier pigeon with a woodpecker?
A bird who knocks before he delivers his message.

What do you get when you cross a chicken with a cement-mixer?
A brick layer.

Did you hear about the scientist who crossed a parrot with an alligator?
It bit his arm off and said, 'Who's a pretty boy?'

What do you get if you give a chicken whisky?
Scotch eggs.

Heard the one about the woodpecker?
It's boring.

Why did the owl 'owl?
Because the woodpecker woodpecker.

A small boy noticed a cageful of green parakeets in a pet shop as he and his mother walked past.

The little boy said, 'Look mother, there are some canaries that aren't ripe yet.'

What kind of hens lay electric eggs?
Battery hens.

Why do birds fly south in winter?
Because it's too far to walk.

Why did the farmer call his rooster Robinson?
Because he crew so.

Why is it silly to hold a party for chickens?
Because these days it's difficult to make hens meet.

JOE: 'I once had a parrot for five years and it never said a word.'
BILL: 'It must have been tongue-tied.'
JOE: 'No, it was stuffed.'

One bird said to the other, 'Look, there's Concorde.' The other bird said, 'Gosh, I wish I could fly as fast as that.'
The first bird said, 'You could, if your bottom was on fire.'

What is a certain way to get a wild duck?
Buy a tame one and annoy it.

Why did the chicken cross the road?
For some foul reason.

What do geese eat?
Gooseberries.

My brother thinks he's a chicken. We'd take him to
the doctor but we can't do without the eggs.

T⊙PS
and
Tails

Where
does Tarzan
get his clothes?

How do we
know Moses
wore a wig?

WHAT DID ONE
SOLE SAY TO
THE OTHER?

A man goes into a butcher's shop and says, 'Have you got a sheep's head?'
The butcher replies, 'No, it's just the way I part my hair.'

Why did the bald man stick his head out of the window?
   To get some fresh air (hair).

What did one ear say to the other ear?
Between us we need a haircut.

What do barbers study?
Short cuts.

What's the difference between a burglar and a man wearing a wig?
One has false keys and the other has false locks.

What is a complete waste of time?
Telling a bald man hair-raising stories.

What man would you always take your hat off to?
A barber.

A man walked into a shop and asked for a wig. After choosing his wig the shopkeeper said, 'That will be £8.00 with tax (tacks).'
The reply was, 'It's all right, I'll glue it on.'

How do we know that Moses wore a wig?
>*Because sometimes he was seen with Aaron and sometimes without.*

What did the hat say to the scarf?
>'*You hang around while I go on ahead.*'

'Would you like to buy a pocket calculator, sir?'
'No thanks, I know how many pockets I've got.'

How should you dress on a cold day?
>*Quickly.*

What did one sole say to the other?
>'*Watch out – two heels are following us.*'

CUSTOMER: 'I would like to try on that suit in the window, please.'
ASSISTANT: 'I'm sorry, sir, you'll have to try it on in the changing-rooms like everybody else.'

Where does Tarzan get his clothes from?
>*A jungle sale.*

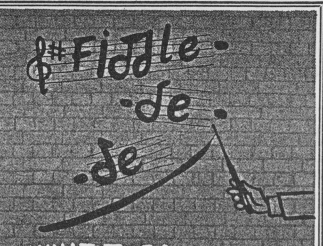

WHAT TUBA
CAN'T YOU PLAY?

what's musical
and handy in a
supermarket?

WHAT'S MUSICAL
AND HOLDS 36
GALLONS OF
BEER?

PIANO TUNER: 'I've come to tune your piano.'
MAN: 'But we didn't send for you.'
TUNER: 'No, but your neighbours did.'

Did you hear about the musician who spent all his time in bed?
Yes, he wrote sheet music.

What sort of musical instrument did Ancient Britons play?
The Anglo Saxophone.

What's musical and handy in a supermarket?
A Chopin Liszt.

What were the Chicago gangster's last words?
Who put that violin in my violin case?

What do you get when a piano falls down a mine?
> *A flat miner.*

What's musical and can hold thirty-six gallons of beer?
> *A Barrel Organ.*

What song was sung when the yacht exploded?
> *Pop goes the wee sail.*

What holds five dozen keys but never opens a door?
> *A piano.*

What tuba can't you play?
> *A tuba toothpaste.*

Once there was a man who wouldn't stop singing. He was told that if he didn't keep quiet, he would be put in front of the firing squad, but he still carried on. Preparations were made for his execution. Before the soldiers aimed, the man asked if, as his last wish, he might sing a song. This was granted and he began to sing a song entitled '10,000 Green Bottles'.

What is the keynote of good manners?
> *'B natural.'*

What pets make the most noise?
> *Trumpets.*

What's the best birthday present?
> *Difficult question, but a drum takes a lot of beating.*

Batty Books and WILY WORDS

WHEN DID THE FIRST TWO VOWELS APPEAR?

why is the letter "E" LAZY?

WHAT FOUR LETTERS FRIGHTEN A THIEF?

OLYMPIC GAMES by *Arthur Letics*

HOW TO MAKE HONEY by *B. Keeper*

EASY MONEY by *Robin Banks*

IN THE COUNTRY by *Theresa Greene*

MARY CRISSMUSS by *Miss L. Toe*

GUNFIRE by *R. Tillery*

TIME TO EAT by *Dean R. Bell*

LONG WALK by *Miss D. Bus*

FITTING CARPETS by *Walter Wall*

ROUND THE WORLD by *Sir C. Umference*

THE GREAT DESCENT by *Aileen Dover*

THE DOGS' DINNER by *Nora Bone*

THE HAUNTED HOUSE by *Hugo First*

JUNGLE ANIMALS by *Ann T. Lope*

BABY SITTING by *Justin Casey Howls*

A HOLE IN MY BUCKET by *Lee King*

What's the longest word in the dictionary?

> *'Smiles', because it has got a mile between the first and last letters.*

Why is elastic one of the longest words in the dictionary?

> *Because it stretches.*

Where does Thursday come before Wednesday?

> *In the dictionary.*

What's the definition of illegal?

> *A sick bird.*

What's the definition of an archaeologist?

> *A man whose career is in ruins.*

What's the definition of a volcano?

> *A mountain with a hiccup.*

What's the definition of minimum?

> *A very small mother.*

What's the blackest letter in the alphabet?

> *O, because it has been twice placed in soot.*

Why are the letters N and O important?

> *We can't get 'on' without them.*

What is the end of everything?

> *The letter G.*

I occur once in every minute, twice in every moment but not once in a hundred thousand years. What am I?
>
> *The letter M.*

Which is easier to spell, seventeen or eighteen?
>
> *Seventeen because it's spelt with more E's (ease).*

What four letters frighten a thief?
>
> *O.I.C.U.*

What begins with a T, ends with a T and has T in it?
>
> *Teapot.*

What's the most unfortunate letter in the alphabet?
>
> *The letter U – whenever there's trouble you'll always find U in the middle of it.*

Why is an island like the letter T?
>
> *It's in the middle of water.*

Why is the letter E lazy?
>
> *Because it's always in bed.*

When did the first two vowels appear?
>
> *Before U or I were born.*

Take away my first letter, take away my second letter, take away all my letters and I still remain the same. What am I?
>
> *A postman.*

Funny Fuzz

THE POLICE ARE LOOKING FOR A MAN WITH ONE EYE CALLED MURPHY—

Where do policemen live?

What happens if you dial 666?

What does 36" make in Edinburgh?

MICHAEL: 'Could you tell me the way to Bath?'
POLICEMAN: 'I always use soap and water.'

LADY TO POLICEMAN: 'Send for the flying squad, please.
I've lost my canary.'

A policeman saw an old man walking towards him pulling along behind him a brick on a lead. The policeman thought, 'Poor chap's obviously a bit simple, I'd better go and humour him.'

So when the two met, the policeman said to the old man, 'Hello, I like your dog, what's his name?'

The old man looked at the policeman and said 'It's not a dog, it's a brick,' and the policeman was taken aback.

'Oh,' he said, 'I'm sorry. I thought you were a bit simple,' and he turned and walked on.

The old man looked at the brick and said, That fooled him, didn't it, Rover?'

A pet shop in Manchester was burgled today. Police cannot find the thief because there aren't any leads.

NEWSCASTER: 'Two prisoners escaped today. One is seven feet tall and the other is four feet six inches. Police are looking high and low for them.'

NEWSCASTER: 'A man found guilty of sticking green stamps on his insurance card was given a three-month jail sentence and an electric kettle.'

BILL: 'The police are looking for a man with one eye called Murphy.'

WILL: 'What's his other eye called?'

How do police give chase under water?
> *They use a squid car.*

Why did the policewoman climb the tree?
> *Because she was in the Special Branch.*

BOY: 'When I grow up I'm going to be a policeman and follow my father's footsteps.'
FRIEND: 'I didn't know your dad was a policeman.'
BOY: 'He's not, he's a burglar.'

POLICEMAN: 'I'm sorry, sonny, but you need a permit to fish here.'
BOY: 'Thanks, but I'm doing pretty well with a worm.'

'Could you see me across the road, constable?'
> *'I could see you a mile away, ma'am!'*

If I dug a hole in the middle of the road, what would come up?
> *A policeman.*

What does 36 inches make in Edinburgh?
> *One Scotland yard.*

What happens when you cross a police constable with a ghost?
> *You get an inspectre.*

What do you call a flying policeman?
> *A heli-copper.*

What do policemen have in their sandwiches?
> *Truncheon meat.*

What's the definition of copper plates?
Policeman's false teeth.

What happens if you dial 666?
A policeman comes along upsidedown.

Where do policemen live?
999 Letsbe Avenue.

What does a cashier in a police station do?
He counts coppers.

Why are policemen strong?
Because they can hold up traffic.

Why did the policeman cry?
Because he couldn't take his panda to bed.

"SQUEALING WHEELS

ARE MY INDICATORS WORKING?

When is a car not a car?

What's big, hairy and flies at 2,000 m.p.h?

WHAT'S RED, RUNS ON WHEELS AND EATS GRASS?

"PORTER, HOW LONG WILL THE NEXT TRAIN BE?"

What kind of ears does a train have?
Engineers.

SAM: 'One of my ancestors died at Waterloo.'
PHILIP: 'Really? Which platform?'

What's the difference between a train driver and a teacher?
One minds the train and the other trains the mind.

Where do Volkswagens go when they get old and tattered?
The Old Volks home.

'Come in Number 9. Your time is up.'
'But we've only got eight boats, sir.'
'Oh, are you in trouble Number 6?'

When is a car not a car?
When it has turned into a lay-by.

What's big, hairy and flies at 2,000 m.p.h.?
King Kongcord.

Are my car indicators working?
Yes, no, yes, no, yes . . .

What do you get if you cross a pig with the M1?
A road hog.

MAN: 'A return ticket, please.'
RAILWAY CLERK: 'Where to?'
MAN: 'Why back here of course.'

What transport is safest in a storm?
A bus, it has a conductor.

What is a Fjord?
A Norwegian motor car.

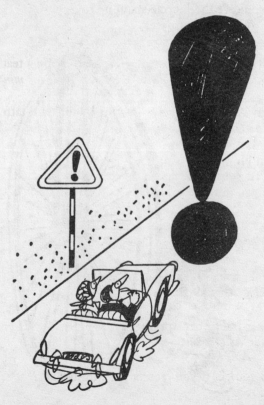

PASSENGER: 'Porter, how long will the next train be?'
PORTER: 'Six carriages, sir.'

Have you heard about the man who drove his car over a cliff?
> *He wanted to test the air-brakes.*

What's red, runs on wheels, and eats grass?
> *A bus.*

PS. I lied about the grass.

Why couldn't the bicycle stand up?
> *Because it was tyred.*

Do you know why the man drove his car into a lake?
He was trying to dip the headlights.

BUS CONDUCTOR: 'This penny you have just given me has a hole in it.'
BOY: 'So has this ticket you have just given me.'

Customer in hurry at a garage: 'Don't bother with the petrol, just give me the stamps.'

Why are the goods in a ship like petrol?
They both make a car go.

What's a twack?
Something a twain runs on.

What has one horn and gives milk?
A milk lorry.

Which driver never commits a traffic offence?
A screwdriver.

Why can't a steam engine sit down?
Because it has a tender behind.

Pun and Games

What ring is square?

What goes putt-putt-putt-putt-putt-putt-p...

What is a big game hunter?

Who was the fastest runner in history?
Adam. He was the first in the human race.

What is a big game hunter?
A man who loses his way to a football match.

CAPTAIN: 'Why didn't you stop the ball?'
GOALIE: 'What do you think the nets are for?'

Who gets the most kicks out of his job?
A footballer.

What has twenty-two legs and two wings but cannot fly?
  A football team.

FOOTBALLER: 'I have a good idea to improve the team.'
MANAGER: 'Good, are you leaving?'

What team's footballers have never met each other before the game?
  Queen's Park Strangers.

In what game do you need to wear ear-plugs?
  Tennis, because you can't play without a racket.

How do you service a pogo-stick?
  Give it a spring-clean.

'Still on crutches, old man?'
'Yes, I'll never jump over the net at table-tennis again.'

What goes putt-putt-putt-putt?
A bad golfer.

What ring is square?
A boxing-ring.

What do miners play in the pit?
Mineopoly.

What does a winner lose in a race?
His breath.

What race is never run?
A swimming race.

How do you start a jelly race?
Say 'get set'.

How do you start a Teddy race?
Ready, Teddy, go.

How do you start a pudding race?
Say go.

How do you start a flea race?
One, two, flea, go.

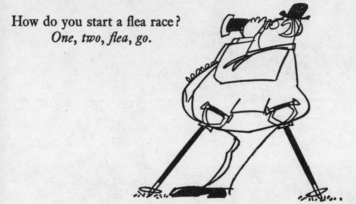

Announcement at a village match: 'For the benefit of the players, here are the names of the spectators.'

Country cackles

WHERE DO FROGS KEEP THEIR SAVINGS?

What are assets?

What did the beaver say to the tree?

How do you catch a squirrel?

WHY IS A KETTLE CALLED AN ANIMAL?

WHAT DID THE RAM SAY TO HIS GIRL FRIEND?

Why is a farmer cruel?
> *Because he pulls the corn by its ears.*

Why was the farmer cross?
> *Because someone trod on his corn.*

Where do cows go on holiday?
> *Moo York.*

What do you call a cow eating grass?
> *A lawn mooer.*

What's the difference between an angry audience and a cow with laryngitis?
> *One boos madly and the other moos badly.*

What do you call a bull asleep on the ground?
> *A bulldozer.*

What did the bull say to the cow?
> *When I fall in love it will be for heifer.*

Once a farmer had a large hay field. His son was not happy in the country, so he moved to town to look for a job. The only job he could get was shining shoes, so now the farmer makes hay while the son shines.

GIRL: 'I say, what a lovely colour that cow over there is.'
BOY: 'It's a jersey.'
GIRL: 'Really, I thought it was his skin.'

What did the ram say to his girlfriend?
  I love ewe.

What do you get if you cross a sheep with a kangaroo?
  A jumper with a pocket.

What are assets?
  Little donkeys.

Why do white sheep eat more than black sheep?
  Because there are more white sheep.

How does a sheep keep warm in winter?
  By central bleating.

Where does a lamb go when he needs a haircut?
  To a baa-baa shop.

Why does a rabbit have a shiny nose?
  Because its powder puff is at the other end.

How do you catch a squirrel?
Climb up a tree and act like a nut.

A man was seen inspecting rabbit holes. What do you think his job was?
A Borough Surveyor.

What did the stag say to his children?
'Hurry up, deers.'

What do you call high-rise flats for pigs?
Sty scrapers.

Why is getting up at four in the morning like a pig's tail?
Because it's twirly (too early).

Why is a pig in a kitchen like a house on fire?
The sooner you put it out the better.

Whatever happened to the piglet who wanted to be in a Shakespeare play?
He ended up as Hamlet.

What did the pig say when the man grabbed him by the tail?
This is the end of me.

What did the beaver say to the tree?
It was nice gnawing you.

Why is a kettle called an animal?
Because it is a water otter.

Where do frogs keep their savings?
In the river bank.

Where do tadpoles go when they lose their tails?
>   *To a retail shop.*

What do you call a frog spy?
>   *A croak and dagger agent.*

What goes croak! croak! when it's misty?
>   *A frog-horn.*

What do you get if you cross a frog and a can of cola?
>   *Croak-a-cola.*

How can you tell which end of a worm is his head?
>   *Tickle his middle and see which end smiles.*

What is a caterpillar?
>   *A worm in a fur coat.*

What's green and highly dangerous?
>   *A caterpillar with a hand-grenade.*

What lies on the ground a hundred feet up in the air?
>   *A centipede lying on its back.*

What's the biggest moth the world has ever seen?
>   *The Giant Hairy Mam Moth.*

What comes out of a wardrobe at a hundred miles an hour?
>   *Stirling Moth.*

Why could mosquitoes be called religious?
>   *First they sing over you and then they prey on you.*

What is a bee?
>   *A little humbug.*

Why do bees have sticky hair?
  Because they have honey combs.

What's worse than being with a fool?
  Fooling with a bee.

Why couldn't the butterfly get into the dance?
  Because it was a moth-ball.

AUKWARD TAILPIECES

What bird is always out of breath?
A puffin.

What's red, white and black?
A sunburnt penguin.

A man was walking in the park and came across a penguin. He took him to a policeman and said, 'I've found this penguin, what should I do?'

The policeman replied, 'Take him to the zoo.'

The next day, the policeman was walking in the same park when he saw the same man, with the penguin. He walked up to him and said, 'Didn't I tell you to take that penguin to the zoo?'

'Yes,' replied the man, 'that's what I did yesterday and today I'm taking him to the movies.'

What's black and white and goes round and round?
  A puffin in a revolving door.

What's black and white, black and white, black and white?
  A penguin rolling down a hill.

List of Contributors

Abel, Frances – *Leeds*
Abram, Anthony – *Preston*
A'court, Tina – *Thetford*
Adamska, Mrs A. – *Preston*
Addison, Christopher –
   Thornton
Alderson, Anne
Allan, Laurie
Anderson, Jayne – *Spalding*
Anderson, Jonathan – *Welling*
Anderson, Linda
Anderson, Neil
Andrews, Pete – *Stalybridge*
Annetts, Neil – *Barnsley*
Apicella, Tina – *Leatherhead*
Archer, Caroline – *Oxford*
Armour, Shona – *Wilmslow*
Arran, Elizabeth
Ash, Marc – *Wantage*
Ashford, Neil and Jane –
   Lechlade
Atkinson, Mrs Hilda –
   Middlesbrough
Atkinson, Yvette – *Oxford*
Austen, B. – *London SW2*
Aynsley, Marion

Baar, Heidi – *Bristol*
Backstrom, Janet – *Aldershot*

Bailey, Debbie – *Sale*
Bailey, Nicola – *Newbury*
Bailey, Pauline – *Bromley*
Bailey, Trevor – *Arundel*
Bain, Alex – *Renfrewshire*
Banester, David – *Ferrybridge*
Barbar, Tracy – *Romford*
Barclay, Susan – *Headington*
Barnett, J. – *Aldershot*
Barr, Deirdre – *Blackburn*
Barrett, Alison – *Kennington*
Bartoletta, Gail – *Salford*
Batchelor, John
Bates, Christopher –
   Scunthorpe
Bath, Michael – *Corby*
Baxter, Anne – *Bathgate*
Bayter, F. B. – *Salford*
Beck, Russell – *Chalfont St Peter*
Beckett, Janine – *Cromford*
Beestone, Lesley – *Leatherhead*
Belfield, Carol – *Worsley*
Benjafield, Tony – *Banbury*
Bennett, Mrs G. M. –
   Crescent School, Oxford
Bennett, Robert – *Bramhall*
Berry, Howard – *Harrow*
Berry, Mike
Betts, James – *Luton*

Bhose, Indra – *St Albans*
Biglin, Melanie –*Hull*
Biles, J. –*Harrow*
Bingham, Tracy – *Ordsall*
Bishop Kirk School, *Oxford*
Black, A. – *Birmingham*
Blackall, G. –
  Burnham-on-Crouch
Blackmore, Mary
Blake, Helen – *Manchester*
Blaney, Mary and Stuart –
  Salford
Bloxham, Lesley and Teresa
Bodwell, Joanne – *Margate*
Boggs, Derek – *London N19*
Bolland, Keith – *Aberdeen*
Bonny, Amanda – *St Albans*
Boone, Alison – *Dumfries*
Booth, Rachel – *Edmonton*
Boulliér, Sophie – *Oxford*
Bowker, Katherine – *Oxford*
Bradburn, Joanne – *Stockport*
Brennan, Terence – *Whitfield*
Bridge, Dawn – *Lever*
Bridges, Linda – *Dennington*
Bright, Glenn – *Market
  Harborough*
Brimble, Pamela
Bristow, Caroline – *Derby*
Bromhead, Amanda – *Oxford*
Brookfield, Julia – *Preston*
Brown, Anne-Marie –
  Bayswater Middle School
Brown, Colin – *Oldham*
Brown, Helen – *Oxford*
Brown, Steven – *Stamford*
Brown, Victor – Bayswater
  Middle School
Browne, Tyronne
Brunt, M. V. – *Cheadle*
Buchanan, John – *Glasgow*
Buckley, Cynthia – *Leamington*
Bull, Brian – *Buxton*
Burdett, Lisa – *Merseyside*

Burgess, Lesley – *Magpie,
  Thames Television*
Burk, Penelope – *Oxford*
Burkitt, Adrian – *Stockport*
Burman, Edward –
  Leatherhead
Burrows, Gillian – *Salford*
Burton, Sandra
Bushell, Pamela – *Manchester*
Butcher, Jackie
Butler, James – *Bradford*
Butler, Kevin
Butler, Susan – *Oxford*

Cale, Norma – *Kinellar*
Campbell, M. – *Leicester*
Carden House School, *Aberdeen*
Cardwell, Robin –
  Edinburgh
Carré, Mark – *Guernsey*
Cartmell, Gary – *Stanley*
Cartwright, Amanda –
  Mansfield
Cawer, Stephen
Cawtwell, Robert –
  Peterborough
Challis, Helen – *Upminster*
Chapman, Mary
Chapman, Sally – *Coltishall*
Charlton, Derek – *Witney*
Charlton, Frank – *Tyne and
  Wear*
Chase, Mandy – *Bishopstoke*
Chorley, Adrian – *Morton,
  Warwicks.*
Clark, Ian – *Kirkintilloch*
Clark, J. – *Sudbury*
Clark, Lionel
Clarke, Jason – *Thamesmead*
Clatworthy, Gary – *Romford*
Cleall, Fiona – *Chipping Norton*
Clegg, Frances – *Worcester*
Clement, Christine –
  Leatherhead

Cleverley, Julie and Andrew
Clough, Michael – *Streatham*
Coatus, Colin – *Newcastle*
Cody, Christopher – *London SE11*
Coldicott, Linda – *Hove*
Colley, Sandra – *Glasgow*
Collins, Richard
Conybeare, Catherine – *Oxford*
Cook, Juliet – *Pinner*
Cook, Tracey
Cooper, Debbie – *Cardiff*
Coplestone, Andrew – *Stoulton*
Corr, Julie and Sarah – *Yoxall*
Corrigan, Vincent – *Manchester 4*
Costen, Debbie – *Benfleet*
Coulson, Heather – *Whitby*
Courtnell, Nicholas
Cousens, Angela – *Stoney Burn*
Cox, Amanda – *Headington*
Craig, Angela – *Wimbourne*
Crane, F. C. – *Walworth*
Crawford, E. M. – *Edinburgh*
Crawford, Kenneth
Creasur, Paul – *Brora*
Creed, Marie – *Wheatley*
Cripps, W. F. – *Waterlooville*
Critchley, David – *Liverpool*
Cronin, Diane – *Denton*
Cross, Jane – *Chester*
Crowther, Leslie – *London*
Cunningham, Fiona – *Greenock*
Curren, Michael – *Earls Barton*
Currie, Walter – Kirkcaldy High School
Cushman, Paul – *Fareham*

Dale, Nicky – *Warrington*
Daley, Marcus – *Ipswich*
Dames, Paul – *Middlesbrough*
Darius, Sandra – *Wantage*
Davidson, Michael – *Aberdeen*
Davidson, Scott – *Willenhall*

Davies, Christine – *Mountain Ash*
Davies, Julia – *Wellingborough*
Davies, Neil and Nigel – *Stourport*
Davies, W. H. – Neston Co. Primary School
Debney, Brett – *Oxford*
Delahunty, Anthony – *Manchester*
Dennie, Nichola — *Barnstaple*
Denny, Margaret – *Taunton*
Derrick, Andrew – *Gloucester*
Dickson, Kevin
Dobson, Jane – *Wakefield*
Doe, Darrel – *Woking*
Dougan, J. – *Belfast*
Downey, Chris – *Manchester*
Downey, Wayne – *Bradford*
Dudman, Joey – *Bristol*
Dugdale, Jeff – *Banff*
Dunion, Gillian
Dunn, Maureen – *Dawlish*
Durrant, Carole A. – *Canvey Island*
Durron, Brenda – *Leeds*

Eastwood, Karen – *Leeds*
Elam, Philip – *Coventry*
Entwhistle family
Erskine, Denise
Esdale, Mrs E. A. – *Leatherhead*
Ettridge, Louise – *Twickenham*
Evans, Debbie – *Bermondsey, SE1*
Evans, John – *Cheadle Hulme*

Fagg, Richard A. – *Maidstone*
Farrell, Jackie – *Chew Magna*
Fawcett, Mrs K. – *Middlesbrough*
Fay, Jane E. – *High Wycombe*
Featherstone, Karen – *Penge*
Fleming, Dawn G. – *Kirriemuir*

Flynn, Sean – *Leatherhead*
Focus on Barton readers – *Oxon.*
Ford, G. – *Liverpool*
Forde, Dawn – *Newbury*
Form V – Crescent School, *Oxford*
Form P – Loreburn Primary School, *Dumfries*
Form 2A and 2N – Millfield School, *Somerset*
Form E1 – St Bartholomews, *Newbury*
Form 3 – St Bridges, *Glasgow*
Form J1A – Cheadle Hulme School
Form Upper VI – St Edmunds Hall, *Liverpool*
Foster, John – *Cleveland*
Foster, Mrs M. – *Cleveland*
Francis, Graham – *Leatherhead*
Freimanis, Paul
Frith, Paul J. – *Mansfield*
Fryer, J. M. – *Benfleet*
Fuller, Elizabeth
Fuller, Stephen – *London N7*

Gallagher, Richard – *Leatherhead*
Gameson, Judith and Paul – *Cheadle*
Gann, Rosemary – *Newbury*
Garbett, K. Mary
Gardner, I. – *Coalpit Heath*
Gardner, Tracey – *London E15*
Gardner, Steven – *Cloughfem, Co. Antrim*
Gargan, Christopher – *Salford*
Garrett, Margot
Garry, G. – *Middlesbrough*
Gaster, Mandy – *Middlesbrough*
Gazzard, Simon
Gee, Christopher – *Barford*
George Heriots School:
  Bell, Stuart
Connelly, Christopher
Halliday, Keith
Henrikson, Evan
Imrie, Steven
Jamieson, Grant
Jones, Chandler
Kennedy, Andrew
Marshall, Keith
Melvin, Fergus
Mitchell, Fraser
Osborne, Robert
Patterson, Kevin
Payne, Simon
Porter, Alisdair
Robinson, Scott
Sorbie, Keith
Sutherland, Robin
Wight, Iain
Williamson, Neil
Zimmo, Basil
Giedroyc, Melanie – *Leatherhead*
Giffin, Hazel – *Oxford*
Gill, Esther
Gillbanks, James – *Liverpool*
Gillett, Gerald – *Newbury*
Gillott, Jane – *Nottingham*
Gingell, Neal
Glover, Gary
Goncalves, Greg – *Tyne and Wear*
Goodfellow, Robin – *Hull*
Goodies, The – *London*
Gooding, Odette – *Barnstaple*
Goodwin, Clare
Gordon, Joyce – *Manchester*
Graham, A. S. – *Wadhurst*
Grant, Joe
Gravell, Pearl – *Wallsend*
Green, Sheila – *Orford*
Greenhalgh, G. M. – *Sidcup*
Greenough, Debera – *Gtr Manchester*
Greer, Elaine

Griffin, Miranda – *Oxford*
Grimston, Mrs Avril – *Yarm*
Grindley, Diane – *Manchester*
Groom, Rachel – *Leatherhead*
Gross, Darrel – *Thurston*
Groves, Harry – *Ashton under Lyne*
Gunning, Mary – *London SE11*

Hadler, Richard – *Newbury*
Hall, Diane – *Rotherham*
Hall, Jacqueline – *Barsham*
Hall, S. A. – *Manchester*
Hall, Stuart – *Tyne and Wear*
Hancock, Julie – *Cwymbran*
Handley, Sue – *Old Trafford*
Hanmer, Carol – *Huyton Roby*
Hardman, David – *Manchester*
Harley, Edwin – *Dudley*
Harris, John
Harris, Kim – *Stratford*
Harrison, Keith – *Helmington*
Harrison, Margaret – *Ashton under Lyne*
Harrison, Simon – *Stoke on Trent*
Hart, Jane – *Witney*
Harvey, Nicola – *Oxford*
Hassain, Sara M. – Crescent School, *Oxford*
Hatchard, Dawn – *Poole*
Havney, Rosemary – *Leatherhead*
Heard, Linda
Heathcote, Wayne – *Stockport*
Hefferan, Glenis and Sue
Helsden, David – *Clapham SW4*
Hewitt, Tom
Heywood, Michael
Hibbert, Amanda – *Dinnington*
Hibbs, Tracie – *Manchester*
Hickey, Karen – *Harlow*
Higgins, Bruce – *Leatherhead*
Higginson, Gaynor – *Wolverhanpton*

Hill, Lisa – *Edgware*
Hindle, Lynne – *Rochdale*
Hindmarshage, Christine
Hitchen, Anthony – *Blackpool*
Hoare, P. R. and class – Bennett Memorial School, *Tunbridge*
Hobbs, Andrew
Hobson, Alan – *Sheffield*
Hodson, Sarah L. – *Oxford*
Hogan, Geraldine – *Rosslare, Co. Wexford*
Holding, Gary – *Gtr Manchester*
Holdsworth, Margaret – *Cleckheaton*
Holgate, Jacqueline – *Edinburgh*
Holland, Ivy and Mark
Holland, Rodney
Holland, Wayne – *Merseyside*
Holliday, Charles – *Glasgow*
Holloway, Philip – *Leatherhead*
Holmes, Derek
Holmes, Jackie – *Devizes*
Holmes, Tony – *Cleveland*
Holt, Richard – *Prestwich*
Hook, Andrew – *Dagenham*
Hooks, Mrs G. – Millfield School, *Somerset*
Hooper, Michele – *Leatherhead*
Hope, Kathryn – *Bury*
Hope, Stan L.
Horistan, Adam – *Cleveland*
Hornby, Abigail
Horsefield, Michelle – *Scarborough*
Hossain, Dina – *Oxford*
Howard, Steven
Howell, Michaela – *Bolton*
Hudson, John – *Macclesfield*
Hudson, Tim – *Middlesbrough*
Hughes, Adrian – *Rhyl*
Hughes, John – *Normanton*
Hughes, Richard – *Worcester*

Hulme family – *Malvern*
Hulme, Janette – *Oldham*
Humphrey, Jacqueline –
   Eastbourne
Hunt, Andrew – *Burnley*
Hunt, Denise – *Clipstone*
Hunt, Mr P. – *Manchester*
Hunt, Susan – *Birmingham*
Hunter, David
Hunter, Hugh – *Dumbarton*
Hutton, Jayne – *Risca, Gwent*
Hyde, Helen – *East Ham E6*

Jackson, A. – *Mablethorpe*
Jackson, Ken – *Manchester*
Jackson, Lorraine – *Braunton*
James, Sarah – Bayswater
   Middle School
James, Susan – *Reading*
Jeffrey, Alan
Jenkins, Jann – *Newcastle
   Emlyn, Dyfed*
Johnson, Andrea – *Bolton*
Johnson, Carol – *Hattersley*
Johnson, Kerry – *Stoke on Trent*
Johnson, Neil – *Stockport*
Jones, Andrew – *Barnsley*
Jones, David
Jones, Howard – *Failsworth*
Jones, Paul – *Port Talbot*
Jones, Sharon – *Cheadle*

Katsapaos, George – *Southgate
   N14*
Kelly, Simon – *Heywood*
Kerfoot, Glyn
Kerr, Michael – *Romford*
Kerry, Shane
Kimberley, Claire –
   Leatherhead
Kimberley Comprehensive,
   Nottingham
   various pupils including:
   Butler, Andrew

Dalton, Richard
Kirk, Neil
Truman, David
King, F. – *Bath*
King, Lesley – *Glasgow*
Kite, Jenny – *Newbury*
Knight, Linda – *Gosport*
Knox, Heather – *Buckhurst Hill,
   Essex*

Lancelot, Mark – *Nelson*
Lattimer, Evelyn – *Gateshead*
Laurence, Simon – *Brighton*
Law, Brian – *Aberdeen*
Lawrence, Paul
Leiper, B. – *Inverurie*
Leisewling, Sarah – *Oxford*
Lennon, Eddie – *London SW1*
Levack, Dominique L. –
   Potters Bar
Lever, Christine – *Northenden*
Levey, Denis
Lewis, Anita – *Borth*
Lewis, Julie
Leylands, Jo'Anne – *Leicester*
Lightfoot, P. E. – *Littlehampton*
Liversidge, Dawn – *Ordsall*
Lloyd, John – *Headington*
Lloyd, Wendy – *Lampeter*
Locke, Karen – *Headington*
Lomanto, Salvatore –
   Leatherhead
Lomas, Anthony – *Salford*
Longmuir, Nathalie – *Dundee*
Lontit, Derek – *Glasgow*
Loosen, Peter – *Newbury*
Loutit, Michael – Kirkcaldy
   High School
Ludbrooke, Anne

Maasz, R. C. – *Oxford*
McAlpin, Kevin and Julie –
   East Ham
McCoy, Lesley – *Doncaster*

McDermott, Joe – *Liverpool*
McDonald, Charlie – *Glenrothes*
McDonald, James – *Petersfield*
McDonald, Michael – *Belturbet*
McDonald, Paul – *Stockton on Tees*
McDonnell, Stephen – *Manchester*
McGee, A. – *Cleveland*
Machin, J. – *London NW10*
McIntyre, Peter – *West Carnforth*
McKay, Denver – *Liverpool*
McKenzie, Neil – *Aberdeen*
McKinlay, Gail – *Falkirk*
McLaren, Nicola – *Rotherham*
McManus, David – *Hartlepool*
McMillan, Ian – *Glasgow*
McNamara, Richard
McQuillan, James
Macrae, Moira – *Ballingry*
Maddock, A. M. – *Llangadog*
Mallabar, Stephen – *Cleveland*
Mansell, Carol – *Chester*
Marks, David – *Muswell Hill*
Marsh, Karen
Marshall, Alison – *Oxford*
Meakin, Paul – *Beeston, Notts.*
Mercer, Andrew – *Stockport*
Mesrie, Daniel
Mett, Elaine – *Rose Hill*
Meyjes, Joanna – *Oxford*
Michaelson-Yeates, Anthea – *Oxford*
Miles, Julie
Miles, Tracy – *Teignmouth*
Miller, Ken
Miller, Tom and Jim – *Wick, nr Bristol*
Mitchell, Janet – *Hattersley*
Mitchell, Mark – *Newcastle under Lyme*
Mitchell, Scott – *Renfrewshire*
Mitchinson, Peter – *Middlesbrough*

Molloy, Kevin – *Slough*
Moore, Estelle
Moore, Joanne – *Leeds*
Morgan, Charlotte E. – *Oxford*
Morris, Samantha
Mouland, Joanne
Mountjoy, Sally
Muhl, Tim – *Bridport*
Mullick Khan, A. – *Oxford*
Munro, Rachael – *Oxford*
Musgrave, Kerry
Musgrave, M. – *Barnsley*

Neston County Primary School, *Wirral*
Nicolson Memorial Manse, *Shetland*
Norris, Paula – *Newbury*

O'Kane, Paula – *Belfast*
Olsen, Ria – *New York*
O'Neill, Daren – *Maidenhead*
Onion, Lisa – *Boreham Wood*
Otten, Mark – *Leatherhead*
Ownsworth, Linda – *Silkstone Common*
Oxbury, Juliet – *Oxford*

Palgrave, Joy – *Norwich*
Paolinelli, Franco – *Newcastle, Co. Down*
Parfoot, Barbara – *Gosport*
Park, Mandy
Parker, Helen – *Fraserburgh*
Parker, Wendy – *Wimbledon*
Parry, Donna – *Middlesbrough*
Paskin, Sian – *Newbury*
Patel, S. R. – *Shepherds Bush*
Pearce, Francesca – *Glasgow*
Pearsall, J. – *Spalding*
Peart, Ian – *Grimsby*
Peck, Shane – *Abingdon*
Pender, Martin – *Wexford, Eire*
Pentland, Keith

Pepperell, Amanda – Bayswater Middle School
Percy, Les – *Rochdale*
Peterson, William – *Glenrothes*
Phipps, Stephen – *Abingdon*
Pickering, Glenton A. – *Peterlee*
Pilkington, Karen
Pinto, Dawn – *South Croydon*
Plant, Debra – *Stoke on Trent*
Potter, Elizabeth – *Chipping Norton*
Potter, Gordon – *Pentabane*
Potter, Karen – *Syston*
Potts, Derek – *Manchester*
Pratley, Louise – *Long Hanborough*
Pratt, Vanessa – *Dover*
Prestwich, Justine – *Oxford*
Price, Andrew – *Newbury*
Pritchard, David
Proctor, John and Stuart – *Stockton on Tees*
Proudfoot, Derek
Pursell, T. – *Horbury*

Quainton, Jackie – *Witney*
Quinn, Hilda – *Portstewart, Eire*

Raddan, Mrs – *Cliftonville, Northants.*
Rainton, Dawn – *Northeft*
Ramsay, Fiona – *Kirkcaldy*
Rankin, Robert – *N. Kilbowie*
Ranson, Humphrey – *Sudbury*
Rattenbury, Zelk – *Dalverton*
Raveh, E. – *Oxford*
Redman, Lorraine – *Poole*
Redshaw, Robert
Rees, Robert – *York*
Reid, Andrew – *Mobberley*
Reid, Beryl – *London*
Retchie, Michael
Reynolds, Stephen – *Denton*
Riddell, David

Riechal, Alison
Ritchie, Michael and Dorothy – *Londonderry*
Rix, Brian – *London*
Roberts, Kenneth
Roberts, Thomas – *Caernarvon*
Robertson family – *Headington*
Robins, J. – *Romford*
Robinson, Andrew – *Hawarden*
Robinson, Stephanie – *Cowley*
Robinson, Steven
Rogan, Paula and Maeve – *Belfast*
Romain, Paul
Roscoe, Simon – *Oldham*
Ross, John J. – *Wotton*
Ross, Valerie
Rossner, Daniel – *Leatherhead*
Roughley, Sandra – *Paignton*
Rowbottom, Karen – *Blackpool*
Rowlands, Louise – *Newbury*
Rudkin, Paul – *Stamford*
Russell, Debbie – *Bath*

Sadak, Shariff
Sadula, Alexander – *Derby*
St Patrick's Primary School, *Stockton on Tees*
Samuels, Lindsay – *Oxford*
Sanders, R. B. – *Folkestone*
Sandiford, Fiona – *Birmingham*
Schofield, Lesley – *Littleborough, Lancs*
Secombe, Harry – *London*
Selby, Teresa – *Galdthorpe*
Semple, Martin – *Leven*
Sergent, Jackie – *Preston*
Sesum, Stana – *Leicester*
Sewell, Fiona – *Headington*
Seymour, Elizabeth – *Kidlington*
Shackleton, Sandra
Sharrock, James – *Prescot*
Shaw, Amanda – *Wantage*

Shaw, Robert – *Sheffield*
Sheader, Paul – *Bolton*
Sheppard, Tina – *Wantage*
Shilton, Robert
Shore, Kathryn – *Abingdon*
Simpson, Elaine – *Richmond*
Singh, Didar – *Southampton*
Singleton, Cindy – *Morionglos*
Smith, Alison – *Timperley*
Smith, D. – *Anstruther*
Smith, Mike – *Altrincham*
Snushall, Louise – *Wisbech*
Soaft, Peter
Somerville, Kevin
Sonart, Sandy
Spence, Audrey
Spencer, Stuart – *Crewe*
Spenser, Jane – *Glasgow*
Speroni, Mrs F.
Spink, Sharon – *Scarborough*
Stanley, Giles and Matthew – *Oxford*
Stanley, Karl
Stephenson, Muriel
Stevens, Brian – *Swinton*
Stevens, Mark
Stevens, Neil
Steventon, Nigel – *Redcar*
Stone, John – *Bristol*
Stone, Paul – *Bristol*
Stratham, Ian – *Rimily*
Street, Abigail
Sutherland, Sarah – *New Marston*
Swain, Annette – *Luton*
Swaincott, Amanda – *Gt Kimble*
Swanscombe School, *Kent*
Sykes, Julie – *Dunford Bridge*

Takacs, Esther – *Oxford*
Tannen, Whitney
Tate, Douglas
Tavener, Mrs M. and class – *Reading*

Taylor, Elspeth – *Stockton*
Taylor, Melanie – *Shipton under Wychwood*
Taylor, Patricia – *Leatherhead*
Taylor, Robert – Kirkcaldy High School
Teasel, Tracy – *Burton on Trent*
Tegg, Antonia – *Plaistow, E13*
Thake, M. – *Stanstead*
Thaker, Paul – *Newport*
Thomas, Lynn – *Walsall*
Thompson, Dean
Thompson, Martin
Thomson, Mark – *Manchester*
Thomson, William – *Edinburgh*
Thorley, Andrew – *Rochdale*
Thorne, Adrian
Todd, Jennifer
Tompkins, Steven J. – *Regis Dunstaple*
Townsend, Debra – *Old Marston*
Trevis, Tracy and Angela
Tunaley, Tracy – *Leicester*
Tunn, M. – *Baldock*
Turnbull, Linda
Turnbull, Steven – *Prudhoe*
Turner, Lucille – *Bournemouth*
Turr, Tristan – *Morley*
Twigg, Horace – *Stoke on Trent*
Tyson, Darren – *Blackbird Leys*

Vesey, Malcolm – *Osbaldwick*
Vosa, Joseph and Isobel – *Botley*
Vowles, Paul and Pam – *Haywards Heath*

Wake, Nichola – *Oxford*
Wald, Karen – *Oxford*
Waldron, Neil – *Antrim*
Walker, Jimmy
Walker, Sheila
Walsham, Stuart – *Hornchurch*
Walter, Carol – *Long Hanborough*

Walton, Bryan – *Newcastle on Tyne*
Ward, Miss L. – *Bedford*
Warren, Russell – *Norwich*
Warrilow, Elizabeth – *Leicester*
Wassell, David – *Fareham*
Waterfield, Denise – *Stretford*
Waterson, Sandra
Watkins, Alison – *Carmarthen*
Watson, Gareth – *Burwood Park*
Watson, Ian – *Charlton*
Watson, Mark – *Benson*
Watson, Yvonne – *Dumfries*
Watt, David
Waudby, Lesley – *Hull*
Webb, Dianne – *Gt Kimble*
Webster, Gary – *Northallerton*
Weinberg, J., S., J., D. and R. – *Harrow*
Weiskrantz, Julia – *Oxford*
Wells, Gillian – *Drayton*
West, Eileen – *Sheffield*
West, Toni-Ann – *Loughborough*
Westerlea School for Spastics, *Edinburgh*
Wheeler, Deborah – *Hull*
Whibley, Stuart – *Bethersden*
White, Christopher – *Birmingham*
White, Jane – *Yelverton*
White, Mike – *Luxford*
White, Nikola – *Teddington*
White, Rita – *Northampton*
White, Samantha – *Oxford*
White, Simon
Whitehead, Margaret – *Bude*
Whitelock, Miss P. – *North Leigh*
Whitfield, Wendy – *Hounslow*
Whitford, Gary – *W. Yorkshire*

Whittaker, Maria – *Portsmouth*
Wickings, Gillian
Wicor Infants School, Form 6
Weir, Matthew – *Leatherhead*
Wilkinson, Linda – *Bristol*
Wilkinson, Wayne – *Tipton*
Williams, Angela – *Havant*
Williams, Audrey – *Swindon*
Williams, Eric – *Stockport*
Williams, Geraint
Williams, Nigel – *Pontypridd*
Williamson, Mark – *Billingham*
Willson, Simon – *Greatstone on Sea*
Wilson, Margaret
Wilson, Mike
Wilson, Philippa – *Doncaster*
Wilson, Wayne – *Southampton*
Winborn, Douglas – *Leatherhead*
Winsborough, Calum
Winter, Darren – *Aberdare*
Wodge, Jonathan – *Hounslow*
Wolf, Jenny – *Halstead*
Wood, David
Woodard, G. C. – *Kings Cross*
Wooding, Lucy
Woodman, Sarah – *Epsom*
Worthington, Norman – *Bryn*
Wosnitzka, Roger
Wren, Sharon – *Bexleyheath*
Wright, David – *Long Hanborough*
Wright, Kev – *Newton le Willows*

Yates, Jackie – *Manchester*
Yudkin, Ruth – *Oxford*

Zimmer, Sharryn

The Annie Who? jokes were contributed by:

Andersen, Sylvia Marie: Whalsay
Andrew, Frazer: Prestwick

Barber, Roderick: Prestwick
Braine, Gemma: Stapleford
Brown, Stuart

Chapman, Chloe: Bromyard
Collcot, Niel
Cox, Paul

Day, Ian: Stapleford

Foote, Paul: Cardiff

Glover, Ruth: Nottingham
Gonzalez, Paula
Grabowski, Peter: Beckenham

Hill, Laura
Hood, Anthony: Stapleford

Irvine, Robbie W.: Symbister

Keeble, Beverley: Wickford
Khan, Naheed: Watford
Khan, M. Yagoot: Watford
Kitchener, Gareth

Lewis, Matthew: Newcastle-upon-Tyne

Marshall, Keith: Whalsay

Marshall, Keith: Whalsay

May, Michelle: Stapleford
Mensh, Daniel

Neale, Natalie: Billericay

O'Juederio, Daniel: Watford

Pearson, Nikki: Nottingham
Penney, Samantha: Rotherhithe

Ridley, Chris: Chiswick
Robson, Luke: Carlisle

Sandison, John Philip: Whalsay
Shaheen, Nasiea: Watford
Simpson, Marie Jane: Symbister
Sloan, Michael

Tabberner, Anthony: Cardiff
Tannahill, Rona: Prestwick
Taylor, Cara: Prestwick
Treglown, Matthew: Northolt

ul-Riaz, Muhammed Wakas: Watford

Walsh, Lee: Cardiff
Whitworth, Adam: Oxford
Williamson, Alison Jane: Whalsay
Williamson, Susan: Shetlands
Willis, Scott: Beckenham
Wolf, Sebastian: Bishops Caundle
Woolhead, Sara: Cardiff

About OXFAM

You've just finished *The Crack-a-Joke Book*, unless you read books from the back in which case you are about to start it. In the book there are jokes about places, about people, about animals. What they all have in common – we hope – is that they make you laugh, or smile, or giggle, or fall about on the floor groaning.

The world needs jokes and laughter: they are some of the ways in which people cope with adversity and make sense of their lives.

The world needs people to get to know each other so that they can share experiences as well as jokes. There are too many things around that just aren't funny – like poverty and hunger and disease and loneliness and fear. Since 1942 OXFAM has been working with poor and powerless people around the world, working for a fairer world.

Here are just a few of the thousands of projects that OXFAM has supported:

In **Jamaica**, *The Groundwork Theatre Company* providing school and community theatre programmes.

In **Togo**, *La Jeunesse en Action pour le Developpement* providing shelter, education and training for children living on the streets in Lome.

In **Indonesia**, *Yasayan Dian Pevtiwi Indonesia* providing a shredding machine for garbage collectors ro recycle plastic.

In **Chile**, *Radio Leon XIII* providing a rural radio news programme for isolated communities and local schools.

There are ways everyone can help to work for a fairer world.

You could:
- give your old books, toys or other things you no longer need to an OXFAM shop
- save stamps or coins for OXFAM (drop them off at an OXFAM shop)
- organize (with your friends and some adults) a jumble sale or bring-and-buy sale to raise money to help OXFAM
- talk to other people – your friends, your parents, the rest of your

bring-and-buy sale to raise money to help OXFAM

- talk to other people – your friends, your parents, the rest of your family – about ways of working for a fairer world and get yourself and them involved
- refuse to give up on the world.

If you want to know more about OXFAM write to us at:

for England: OXFAM, 274 Banbury Road, Oxford OX2 7DZ

for Ireland: OXFAM, 52–54 Dublin Road, Belfast BT2 7HN
          OXFAM, 202 Lower Rathmines Road, Dublin 6

for Scotland: OXFAM, 14 Royal Crescent, Glasgow G3 7SL

for Wales: OXFAM, 46–48 Station Road, Llanishen, Cardiff CF4 5LU

for Australia: Community Aid Abroad, 156 George Street, Fitzroy, Victoria 3065

for Belgium: OXFAM Belgique, 39 Rue du Conseil, 1051 Bruxelles

for Canada: OXFAM Canada, 250 Laurier Avenue W, Room 301, Ottawa, Ontario K1P 5J6

for Hong Kong: OXFAM, Ground Floor – 3B, June Garden, 28 Tung Chau Street, Tai Kok Tsui, Kowloon, Hong Kong

for Quebec: OXFAM Quebec, 169 Rue St. Paul est, Montreal 127, Quebec H2Y 1G8

for the USA: OXFAM America, 115 Broadway, Boston, Massachusetts 02116

THE GREAT PUFFIN JOKE DIRECTORY
Brough Girling

AARDVARK
Knock, knock!
Who's there?
Aardvark
Aardvark who?
Aardvark a million miles for one of your smiles . . . !

No great directory could start without an aardvark joke. Use this directory to find out what Humpty did with his hat, how to start a jelly race and what the vampire's favourite soup is . . .

Packed with alphabetical fun to keep you and your friends giggling for years, this is the world's funniest A–Z of jokes